全国职业技能英语系列教材

Tour Guide English

导游英语

主 编 王 哲
副主编 李 佳 仇明春
编 委 冯永红 刘凯丽 马慧东

北京大学出版社
PEKING UNIVERSITY PRESS

图书在版编目(CIP)数据

导游英语/王哲主编. —北京:北京大学出版社,2008.9
(全国职业技能英语系列教材)
ISBN 978-7-301-13830-4

Ⅰ.导… Ⅱ.王… Ⅲ.导游-英语-职业教育-教材 Ⅳ.H31

中国版本图书馆CIP数据核字(2008)第067924号

书　　　名:	导游英语
著作责任者:	王　哲　主编
责任编辑:	张建民
标准书号:	ISBN 978-7-301-13830-4/H·1993
出版发行:	北京大学出版社
地　　　址:	北京市海淀区成府路205号　100871
网　　　址:	http://www.pup.cn
电　　　话:	邮购部 62752015　发行部 62750672　编辑部 62759634　出版部 62754962
电子信箱:	zbing@pup.pku.edu.cn
印　刷　者:	北京大学印刷厂
经　销　者:	新华书店
	787毫米×1092毫米　16开本　9.75印张　194千字
	2008年9月第1版　2017年2月第3次印刷
定　　　价:	29.00元

未经许可,不得以任何方式复制或抄袭本书之部分或全部内容。
版权所有,侵权必究
举报电话:(010)62752024　电子信箱:fd@pup.pku.edu.cn

全国职业技能英语系列教材

编委会

顾问
胡壮麟（北京大学）　　　　刘黛琳（中央广播电视大学）

总主编
丁国声（河北外国语职业学院）

编委会名单（以姓氏笔画为序）
丁小莉（山东商业职业学院）
王乃彦（天津对外经济贸易职业学院）
牛　健（中央广播电视大学）
伍忠杰（电子科技大学）
李相敏（河北外国语职业学院）
李恩亮（江苏海事职业技术学院）
张　冰（北京大学出版社）
张九明（开封大学）
张春生（衡水职业技术学院）
陆松岩（江苏城市职业学院）
陈玉华（成都航空职业学院）
林晓琴（重庆电力高等专科学校）
赵　倩（重庆机电职业技术学院）
赵　鹏（北京联合大学）
赵爱萍（浙江水利水电专科学校）
赵翠华（承德民族师范高等专科学校）
胡海青（南京交通职业技术学院）
贾　方（辽宁装备制造职业技术学院）
黄宗英（北京联合大学）
崔秀敏（承德石油高等专科学校）
蒋　磊（河南商业高等专科学校）
程　亚（江西景德镇陶瓷学院）
黎富玉（成都航空职业学院）
潘月洲（南京工业职业技术学院）
Martin Fielko (Cornelsen Press GmbH & Co. KG)

总　序

我国高职高专教育的春天来到了。随着国家对高职高专教育重视程度的加深,职业技能教材体系的建设成为了当务之急。高职高专过去沿用和压缩大学本科教材的时代一去不复返了。

语言学家 Harmer 指出:"如果我们希望学生学到的语言是在真实生活中能够使用的语言,那么在教材编写中接受技能和产出技能的培养也应该像在生活中那样有机地结合在一起。"

教改的关键在教师,教师的关键在教材,教材的关键在理念。我们依据《高职高专教育英语课程教学基本要求》的精神和编者做了大量调查,秉承"实用为主,够用为度,学以致用,融类旁通"的原则,历经两年艰辛,为高职高专学生编写了这套专业技能课和实训课的英语教材。

本套教材的内容贴近工作岗位,突出岗位情景英语,是一套职场英语教材,具有很强的实用性、仿真性、职业性,其特色体现在以下几个方面:

1. 开放性

   本套教材在坚持编写理念、原则及体例的前提下,不断增加新的行业或岗位技能英语分册作为教材的延续。

2. 国际性

   本套教材以国内自编为主,以国外引进为辅,取长补短,浑然一体。目前已从德国引进了某些行业的技能英语教材,还将从德国或他国引进优秀教材经过本土化后奉献给广大师生。

3. 职业性

   本套教材是由高职院校教师与行业专家针对具体工作岗位、情景过程共同设计编写。同时注重与行业资格证书相结合。

4. 任务性

   基于完成某岗位工作任务而需要的英语知识和技能是本套教材的由来与初衷。因此,各分册均以任务型练习为主。

5. 实用性

本教材注重基础词汇的复习和专业词汇的补充。适合于在校最后一学期的英语教学，着重培养和训练学生初步具有与其日后职业生涯所必需的英语交际能力。

本教材在编写过程中，参考和引用了国内外作者的相关资料，得到了北京大学外语编辑部的倾力奉献，在此，一并向他们表示敬意和感谢。由于本套教材是一种创新和尝试，书中瑕疵必定不少，敬请指正。

丁国声

教育部高职高专英语类专业教学指导委员会委员

河北省高校外语教学研究会副会长

河北外国语职业学院院长

2008 年 6 月

编写说明

　　本教材是在"全国职业技能英语系列教材"总主编、教育部高职高专英语教学指导委员会委员、河北外国语职业学院院长丁国声教授及北京大学出版社张冰主任的主持下,组织全国各地的二十余位英语教学专家讨论编写的,是一本以服务职业培训为原则,将实用性、灵活性的理念融入到具体的内容当中的技能教材。本教材是北京大学出版社出版的全国职业技能英语系列教材的一个组成部分,特点是注重职业仿真环境下工作语言情景的导入,让学生在了解岗位主要流程、工作内容、工作职责、相关知识、文化背景和职业操守的同时,达到能运用英语自如应对涉外工作的目的。

　　《导游英语》是为英文导游编写的一本实训课教材,适用于英文导游专业、涉外旅游专业、旅游英语专业实习和上岗前进行职业培训。本书以导游服务程序为线索,围绕导游服务的核心内容即导游讲解服务进行任务型教学。全书共十个单元,按照旅游项目进行分类,包括古都游、宗教游、园林艺术游、自然山水游等,涉及全国著名旅游胜地。通过导游示范、模拟讲解、现场演练和导游词创作四个教学环节,使即将成为导游的人员了解中国传统文化,熟悉导游服务程序和规范,掌握导游讲解内容和技巧,培养导游员处理突发事件的能力和导游词创作能力。本书不仅可以用作涉外旅游专业的实训教材,同时可作为导游员从事导游服务工作的指导用书。

　　本书遵循项目导向和实境教学理念,融话题、交际功能和语言结构为一体,渗透文化背景知识和学习策略,突出真实职场情境,实施语言项目,实现以人为本、以学生为中心的教学理念,形成一套循序渐进、生活化的学习程序和详尽、科学、严谨的自我评价体系,让不同层次的学习者各有所获、各有所得。该书是一本以项目为载体,着重培养学生自主创新能力和与人交往和合作能力的实训教材。

　　本书由王哲、仇明春、李佳、冯永红、刘凯丽、马慧东参加编写,河北旅游职业学院李军、北京第二外国语学院副教授王向宁及国旅总社资深专家对本书进行了审阅,王哲博士最后统稿,凝聚了行业专家及一线教师的心血和智慧。特别要说明的是该书大部分图片由著名摄影家魏洪如先生提供,部分图片由本书作者在实训基地拍摄,在此表示衷心感谢。

　　因时间仓促,编者水平所限,本书疏漏之处在所难免,恳请各位专家及广大读者批评指正,以使本书不断完善。

CONTENTS

Unit 1	Receiving the Guests	1
Unit 2	On the Way to Hotel	13
Unit 3	Arriving at the Hotel	25
Unit 4	Talking about Tour Arrangement	35
Unit 5	City Tour and Ancient Capitals	46
Unit 6	Chinese Ancient Gardens	59
Unit 7	Humane Landscapes	72
Unit 8	Religious Temples	87
Unit 9	Natural Landscapes	101
Unit 10	Seeing-off the Guests	113
Appendix	Peer's Assessment Form	123
Vocabulary		124
Answer Key		129

Unit 1 Receiving the Guests

AIMS

- To understand the basic preparations before taking the tour group
- To understand what to do before and upon the arrival of the tour group
- To find ways to improve your guiding skills and performance
- To master the basic relating words and expressions of greeting people
- To learn some traditional Chinese festivals

START-UP

Make a list of the basic preparations before taking a tour group. Can you add more in the following chart?

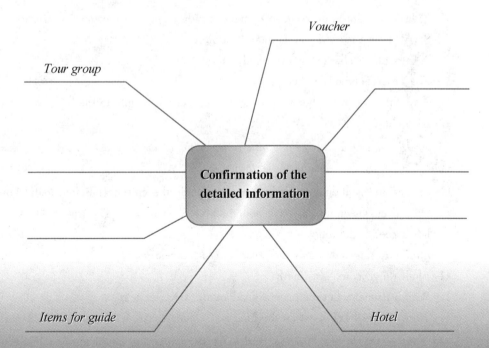

1 **Read the following conversation and answer the questions.**

Receiving the Tourists at the Airport

G: Li Yang   T: Tourist   L: Tour Leader

(*Li Yang is a tour guide in* China International Travel Service (CITS). *She is at the airport and to meet the tour group from the United States. She stands at a visible place of the* exit, *holding a sign highly. The flight arrives. John Smith is the* tour leader.)

G: Excuse me, are you Mr. John Smith, the tour leader from the Sunshine Travel Service in Los Angeles?

T: Yes, I am.

G: I'm Li Yang, the local guide from China International Travel Service, Beijing branch.

L: Glad to meet you.

G: Glad to meet you, too, Mr. Smith. Welcome to China and welcome to Beijing.

L: Thank you.

G: Mr. Smith, could you tell me if everyone in the group has come?

L: All except one. Joseph Brown cancelled the trip without an advanced notice because of an emergency. So, in this group there are 29 members together, including me.

G: That's all right, but we have to make a little change in the room arrangements.

L: Sorry to have caused you so much trouble.

G: No trouble at all. And is everybody here?

L: En. Yes, everybody is here.

G: Now shall we go to check the baggage and get our people to the bus, Mr. Smith?

L: All right.

(*After Li Yang and Mr. John Smith finish with all the baggage, Li Yang leads the tour group to the bus outside the entrance.*)

G: Ladies and gentlemen, our bus is just outside the entrance. Before getting on the bus, if anyone wants to wash your hands, please do so. The washroom is on the left corner of the lobby.

(*Ten minutes later, it seems that everybody has come back.*)

G: Shall we go now, Mr. Smith?

L: Wait a moment. Let me have a headcount... OK, let's go.

G: Here we are! Let's get on the bus.

(*Li Yang stands by the bus door and helps the tourists to board the bus. Finally, he boards the bus, too. The bus departs from the airport to the hotel.*)

> **VOCABULARY ASSISTANT**
>
> exit 出口　　　　　　　　　　tour leader 领队
> China International Travel Service (CITS) 中国国际旅行社

1. Which travel agency is Li Yang from?
   _____

2. Where are the guests from?
   _____

3. How to meet the guests at the airport?
   _____

4. How to introduce yourself to the guests?
   _____

5. What should you do before meeting the guests?
   _____

2　Fill in the gaps with a suitable word from the box. Change their forms if necessary.

arrangement	emergency	depart from	corner	international
headcount	visible	entrance	check	branch

1. Li Yang is a tour guide in China _____ Travel Service (CITS).
2. She stands at a _____ place of the exit, holding a sign highly.
3. I'm Li Yang, the local guide from China International Travel Service, Beijing _____.
4. Joseph Brown cancelled the trip without an advanced notice because of an _____.
5. We have to make a little change in the room _____.
6. Now shall we go to _____ the baggage?
7. Finally, he boards the bus, too. The bus _____ the airport to the hotel.
8. Let me have a _____... OK, let's go.
9. Ladies and gentlemen, our bus is just outside the _____.
10. The washroom is on the left _____ of the lobby.

3　Talk about the situation and tell how to meet the guests at the airport.

Z: Zhang Yang, the tour guide from CYTS
S: John Smith, the tour group leader from Australia
W: Wang Hong, the manager from CYTS

Z: Excuse me, are you Mr. John Smith from the MRB Travel Agency in Australia?
S: Yes, I am.
Z: I'm Zhang Yang, your local guide from CYTS, Beijing Branch.
S: How do you do, Miss Zhang?
Z: How do you do? Welcome to Beijing.
S: Thank you.
Z: Mr. Smith, May I introduce our manager, Mr. Wang to you?
S: Yes, nice to meet you, Mr. Wang.
W: Nice to meet you, too, Mr. Smith. Welcome to China.
S: Just call me John. First name is more friendly than surname, isn't it?
W: Yes, you are right.
Z: Are you all here, John?
S: Yes, we are all here.
Z: Ok. Let's go. This way, please. Our bus is in the parking lot across the street.
W: Did you have a good flight? Did you fly directly from Australia to Beijing?
S: Yes, thank you. The flight was very good and the service was excellent. It took just over 11 hours non-stop from Australia.
W: Good. Is it your first time to visit Beijing?
S: Yes, it is such a beautiful city.
Z: Well, in that case, we shall try to make your visit as pleasant as possible as we can, so that you will take home happy memories. Fortunately, here you can enjoy nice climate, spring is the best season in Beijing.
S: We are so lucky.
Z: If you have any problems, please let me know. I will try my best to help you.
S: Thank you.
Z: Here we are! Let's get on the bus.

4 Read the following information and answer the questions.

Being a tour guide, before you receive a tour group, you must study the reception program carefully as early as you can. The more carefully you study it, the more successful your guiding will be. Receiving the tourists is the first step in your guiding job. So you should make sure of all the detailed information to the reception program (including the information of the tour group, tourists, arrival & departure time, itinerary, hotels, restaurants, transportation, vouchers, items for the guide and the tour group, etc.).

■ Look at the chart below and discuss what you should pay attention to.

The tour group	Name and code of this group, contacting person and telephone number of the organizing travel agency, number of the tourists, names of the tour leader and the national guide, language, etc.
The tourists	Name, nationality, gender, date of birth, religious belief, occupation, special requests, etc.
Itinerary	Arriving and departing times, transportation, hotels and rooms, restaurants and meals, scenic spots, meetings, banquets, etc.
Vouchers	Number and price of the entrance tickets. Flight tickets: (1) For international flights, confirm the tickets 72 hours ahead of departure. (2) For domestic flights, confirm the tickets 48 hours ahead of departure.
Items for guiding	Tour guide certificate, flag, louder speaker, travel schedule, etc.

■ Key points for the tour guide to follow before the arrival of the tour group.

1. Confirm the expected arriving time before departing.
2. Contact the bus driver and travel with the bus to the airport.
3. Arrive at the airport 30 minutes ahead of the expected arriving time.
4. Confirm the parking lot.
5. Reconfirm the exact arrival time at the airport.
6. Contact the porter and inform him of the destination of luggage.
7. Stand at a highly visible place of the exit holding a sign.

■ Key points for the tour guide to follow upon the arrival of the tour group.

1. Meet the tour group and contact the tour leader.
2. Check the name, code of the tour group and the number of tourists.
3. Check if all the luggage have been claimed and collected by porter for transfer to the bus.
4. Show the tour group to the bus and board the bus.
5. The guide should stand by the door and have a headcount silently.

UNIT 1 RECEIVING THE GUESTS

> **VOCABULARY ASSISTANT**
>
> the reception program 接待计划
> itinerary 旅行计划；旅游线路
> gender 性别
> tour guide certificate 导游证
> contact 联系
> destination （旅游）目的地
> hold a sign 手举接站牌
>
> arrival & departure time 抵离时间
> voucher 票据
> entrance tickets 门票
> confirm 确认
> depart 出发
> porter 行李员
> have a headcount 清点人数

1. Being a local guide, what should you do before the arrival of the tour group?
   _____

2. What should a tour guide do at the airport upon the arrival of the tour group?
   _____

3. What is the first step in your guiding job?
   _____

4. What should you study before you receive a tour group?
   _____

5. What detailed information should you make sure?
   _____

6. What information should you know about the tour group?
   _____

7. What is an itinerary?
   _____

8. What is a voucher?
   _____

9. What should you check when you meet the guests?
   _____

10. What should you do after meeting the guests?
    _____

5 **Try to fill in the following chart about the procedure of meeting the guests at the airport.**

1. Check and confirm the reception program information.	8.
↓	↑
2. Contact the bus driver and travel with the bus to the airport.	7.
↓	↑

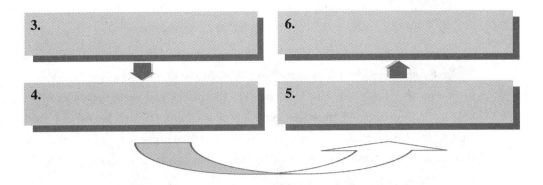

6 Rewrite the following passage into a dialogue and practice with your partners.

English tour guides are similar to diplomats of the people. They directly contact foreign visitors, so their quality and service play decisive roles in the development of tourism industry in China. Their speeches and behaviors directly influence foreign visitors' mood in travelling. In a sense, their duties are to try their utmost to make foreign visitors enjoy their trip during the travel and at the same time let them understand China's history, geography, customs and cultural tradition better through their interpreting and efforts. Therefore, tour guides should be the spirit of mountains and rivers, the envoys of friendship, the disseminators of culture and civilization of the motherland and the moral of socialism. If a tour guide's service is satisfactory, foreign visitors would have a good impression of China for other sights and furthermore, they would urge others to come along to see China with their own eyes. A Travel Agency would, of course, employ as many such competent and qualified English tour guides as possible so as to make their business thrive with each passing day.

English tour guides should be able to act as attendants, publicity agents and defenders while accompanying foreign visitors. So, they should have a perfect mastery of our Party's policies and political ideology, foreign language and relevant knowledge. They must be honest and upright, prudent and careful in their work, diligent and assiduous in their working style. To be more specific, tour guides must keep in mind the following aspects:

1. Sincerity

In treating foreign tourists, tour guides must be sincere, dealing with them like real friends. The tour guides should avoid doing anything to fool foreigners in matters of price, itinerary and schedule. Once the guide is found cheating or hypocritical or telling a lie, the guide would enjoy no prestige as well as trust from foreign friends.

2. Timing

Timing is important to be a guide as the tour is usually well planned and scheduled. Generally speaking, a trip lasts for ten to fifteen days, so tour guides must go out of their ways to observe the schedule and visit the places and scenic spots as scheduled unless some unexpected situations come up or something urgent forces tour guides to change the itinerary. Tour guides should try to arrange every activity with in a time limit so as to let the tourists see China and enjoy themselves as much as possible.

3. Giving Information Ahead

According to the customs of westerners, everything must be properly arranged and informed beforehand. If you want to visit a foreigner, you have to make an appointment with him or her in advance, otherwise, you would interrupt his or her privacy. That is considered to be rude and impolite. It is the same case with a tour guide. Tour guides must always remember that whenever they want to do something or change the plan, they must give the information ahead so as to prepare tourists for the activity of any sort.

4. Helpful

Tour guides should always get ready for helping foreign visitors, especially old lady or an elderly gentleman who is too fat or too old to carry a heavy case or get on a chartered bus, tour guides should give them a hand. This little favor done to tourists would earn some reputation to the Travel Service and in the log run would attract more foreign visitors.

7 **Cultural Salon: Read the following passage, try to get some cultural knowledge about *Traditional Chinese Festivals* and answer the questions.**

Traditional Chinese festivals are important part of Chinese culture. All the traditional festivals in China are based on the Chinese lunar calendar. They were often connected with ancient calendars, astronomy and mathematics. The formation of traditional Chinese festivals is a long process. Solar term is a main factor in forming traditional festivals. According to the traditional Chinese calendar, a year is divided into 24 points, which can accurately show seasonal changes and acts as a basic guidance system for agricultural production. Festival activities always reflect people's spirit and life.

China has many ethnic groups. Different ethnic groups have different festivals. Even on the same festival, they follow different customs. Here we introduce some important and commonly celebrated festivals. These traditional festivals are precious cultural heritage for the Chinese.

The Spring Festival is the most important festival for Chinese people and marks the beginning of the Chinese Lunar New Year. In Chinese, we also say Guo Nian. The Spring Festival starts from the first day of the lunar year, the celebration usually lasts for weeks. This is usually in late January or early February. On the night of New Year's Eve, Chinese families come together for a celebration dinner. No matter how far away from home a person is, he will try to get home in time for the dinner. Some families will also prepare Jiao Zi, Chinese dumplings stuffed with meat and vegetables. Very early the next morning, children greet their parents and receive their presents in terms of cash wrapped up in red paper packages. Then, the family starts out to say greetings from door to door.

The Lantern Festival falls on the 15th day of the 1st lunar month. Watching lanterns is the important activity in this festival. Lanterns of various shapes and sizes are hung in the streets, attracting countless visitors. "Guessing lantern riddles" is an essential part of the Festival. People will eat Yuan Xiao on this day, so it is also called the Yuan Xiao Festival. Yuan Xiao also has another name, Tang Yuan which has a similar pronunciation with "Tuan Yuan", meaning reunion.

The Dragon Boat Festival falls on the 5th day of the 5th lunar month. There is a legend about the evolution of the festival. Qu Yuan was one of ancient China's famous poets. In 278 BC, he heard the news that Qin troops had finally conquered Chu's capital, he plunged himself into the river. It was on the 5th day of the 5th month in the Chinese lunar calendar. After his death, the fishermen sailed their boats up and down the river to look for his body. People threw Zong Zi (pyramid-

shaped glutinous rice dumplings wrapped in reed or bamboo leaves) and eggs into the water to prevent fish or shrimp from attacking his body. That's why people followed the customs such as dragon boat racing, eating Zong Zi on that day.

The Mid-Autumn Festival falls on the 15th day of the 8th lunar month. The festival has a long history. In ancient China, emperors followed the rite of offering sacrifices to the sun in spring and to the moon in autumn. Historical books of the Zhou Dynasty had had the word "Mid-Autumn". Later the ceremony was expanded to common people. They enjoyed the full, bright moon on that day and expressed their thoughts and feelings under it. Now it has become an important festival of China. On the Mid-Autumn Festival, all family members get together and look up at the sky while talking about life. All the people enjoy the full moon and eat moon cakes on that day.

VOCABULARY ASSISTANT

lunar calendar 阴历
solar term 节气
The Spring Festival 春节
The Dragon Boat Festival 端午节

astronomy 天文学
sacrifices 祭品
The Lantern Festival 元宵节
The Mid-Autumn Festival 中秋节

1. What are the traditional festivals in China based on?

2. What will people do on the night of New Year's Eve?

3. What is the important activity in the Lantern Festival?

4. Why did people follow the customs of having dragon boat racing and eating Zong Zi on the Dragon Boat Festival respectively?

5. What did the emperors do on the Mid-Autumn Festival in ancient China?

Further reading: What Is a Tour Guide?

Usually we think of a tour guide as a person that leads tourists to scenic spots and historic attractions and describes the history and culture of these places to the guests. But this is not enough. As a tour guide, you are totally responsible for your guests while they are in China. If you want to be a good tour guide, you must learn many skills.

Firstly, as a tour guide, you must know more about local and national history as well as the culture and traditions of your country. Most tourists come to visit China because of its long history, ancient culture, traditions and arts. So, you should be able to introduce Chinese history and culture to them and describe China both yesterday and today. At the same time, more and more tourists are interested in modern China and the daily life of the modern Chinese people. A knowledgeable tour guide can help tourists understand a great deal about your country and its people. This will make tourists enjoy their stay more. You will also teach them some simple skills, such as how to eat with chopsticks, how a Chinese meal is served. If a member of your group is interested in traditional Chinese art, you can make a reference to Chinese art in your presentations and the group will be much more involved in what you are talking about. You should try to make your presentations interesting and lively so that tourists will be attentive to what you are saying. Don't just talk about historical facts, dates and people's names. Use stories, folk tales and even explanations of Chinese names to make your presentations more interesting. Have jokes with tourists, ask questions and get them in what you are doing. They will enjoy their trip more. Be friendly with your guests and find out what they are interested in. You should always think of yourself as a host. You will help your guests feel welcome in China, they want to enjoy themselves and to be comfortable.

As a tour guide, you should pay more attention to your appearance, manners and attitude. The appearance is the first thing people will notice when they meet you. Your clothes should be clear, neat and suitable for the situation. Your hair should be cut and your face should be shaved. Tourists tend to judge your company and even your country by your appearance. Your manners means how polite and respectful you are. You should be always polite to all guests. If you act poorly, it will reflect badly on both you and your company. The attitude is very important factor in you job. All people are different. They have different education, background, likes and dislikes. Sometimes, it is hard to make all people happy. But your attitude is never secret. People can read it in your face and judge it by your actions. We react against others' attitude if they are strong enough. If the tour guide is bored and not interested, the group will be bored and not interested either. If you are angry about something, you can cause the whole group to develop the attitude.

Your behavior as a tour guide represents not only your personal appearance, but also that of your company and your country. How professional you are will depend on your dress, your ability to use and understand language, your manners and your attitude to your work and your guests.

8 Work in Pairs.

Student A You are a visitor from Britain.

Student B You are a tour guide.
Student B introduces traditional Chinese festivals to Student A below:
The Spring Festival   The Lantern Festival
The Dragon Boat Festival   The Mid-Autumn Festival

9 Supplementary task: Try to make a dialogue about receiving the guests at airport and work with your partners to practice. The teacher and students will remark on your performance.

Unit 2 On the Way to Hotel

AIMS

- To understand how to make a welcome speech
- To understand what to introduce on the way to the hotel
- To find ways to improve your guiding skills and performance
- To master the basic words and expressions
- To know the Chinese local customs

 START-UP

Make a list of main points when you make a welcome speech.

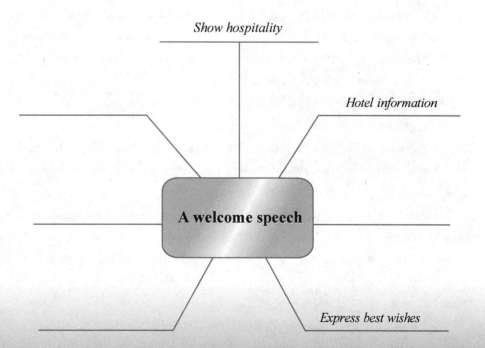

1 **Read the following welcome speech and answer the questions.**

Good afternoon, ladies and gentlemen!

Welcome to China, welcome to Beijing! On behalf of the staff of China International Travel Service, Beijing Branch, please allow me to express our warm welcome to all of you. There is an old saying in China, which goes "Isn't it a great pleasure to have friends coming from afar? " Today, it's an honor for me to meet you and to be of service. Now we are heading to the hotel. Please sit back and relax.

I'm Li Yang from China International Travel Service, Beijing Branch. During your stay in Beijing, I'll be your local guide. You can call me Lee. This is my colleague Mr. Zhang, the national guide. She will travel with you throughout the trip in China. And this is Mr. Wang, our bus driver, he is an experienced driver and has a driving experience of more than 20 years. You have to remember the number of the bus. The bus number is JH-05123. Let me repeat it, JH-05123. When you are in China, we will try our best to make your trip a pleasant and rewarding experience. If you have any questions or problems, please don't hesitate to tell me. My mobile phone number is 13031429999. I would have it on for 24 hours a day. Please contact me whenever you are in need.

You are going to stay in Beijing Hotel, which is a luxurious, five-star hotel, located in the city center Chang'an Street. It will take us about 40 minutes to get there. Now I'd like to remind you to reset your watches. Now it's 5:10 p.m. Beijing time. In China, the whole country adopts Beijing standard time, which is eight hours ahead of Greenwich Mean Time. Oh, I almost forget to inform you that your luggage will be sent to the hotel by another bus, so don't worry about it.

You will stay in Beijing for three days. As the capital of China, Beijing has a long history and a brilliant culture. It is a pleasant place to visit, as well as to do business, to shop, to dine or to be entertained. According to the itinerary, you'll visit the Forbidden City, the Summer Palace, the Temple of Heaven and the Great Wall. They are the world wonders. You can also have a taste of delicious Beijing food, particular the Roast Beijing Duck and Donglaishun Hot Pot. Furthermore, you may enjoy some traditional performances at night, such as Peking Opera, Acrobatic Show.

My dear friends, I sincerely wish you a pleasant and comfortable stay in Beijing. I shall do all I can to make everything easy for you. Enjoy yourselves and good luck! Thank you for your attention.

ON THE WAY TO HOTEL UNIT 2

■ **Key points for a welcome speech.**
1. Express welcome and extend greetings to tourists who have just arrived.
2. Introduce yourself, other tour guides, bus driver and the travel agency you work for.
3. Provide the bus number and your mobile phone number.
4. Show you are willing to offer any help and provide high quality service.
5. Inform the tourists of the hotel information (including its rank, location and facilities etc.).
6. Give a brief introduction of the history, geography, main scenic spots, local dishes, arts and handcrafts, local custom and economy and so on.
7. Last but not the least, express your best wishes to the guests.

VOCABULARY ASSISTANT

local guide 地陪
Greenwich Mean Time 格林尼治标准时间
the Summer Palace 颐和园
acrobatic show 杂技表演
national guide 全陪
the Forbidden City 故宫
the Temple of Heaven 天坛

1. Which travel service is Li Yang from?

2. What's the bus number?

3. How many hours is Beijing standard time ahead of Greenwich Mean Time?

4. According to the itinerary, how many scenic spots will the tourists visit? What are they?

5. What traditional performances may the tourists enjoy at night?

2 **Fill in the gaps with a suitable word from the box. Change their forms if necessary.**

colleague	hesitate	reset	brilliant	furthermore
relax	rewarding	luxurious	adopt	itinerary

1. Now we are heading to the hotel. Please sit back and _____.
2. This is my _____ Mr. Zhang, the national guide. She will travel with you throughout the trip in China.
3. When you are in China, we will try our best to make your trip a pleasant and _____ experience.

4. If you have any questions or problems, please don't _____ to tell me.
5. You are going to stay in Beijing Hotel, which is a _____, five-star hotel, located in the city center Chang'an Street.
6. Now I'd like to remind you to _____ your watches. Now it's 5:10 p.m. Beijing time.
7. In China, the whole country _____ Beijing standard time, which is eight hours ahead of Greenwich Mean Time.
8. As the capital of China, Beijing has a long history and a _____ culture.
9. According to the _____, you'll visit the Forbidden City, the Summer Palace, the Temple of Heaven and the Great Wall.
10. _____, you may enjoy some traditional performances at night, such as Peking Opera, Acrobatic Show.

3 Talk about the situations and make different welcome speeches to the guests.

1. Make a welcome speech to the independent tourists (Mr. & Mrs. Black) from the United States.

2. Make a welcome speech to the tour group from Canada.

3. Make a welcome speech to the international school students from Britain.

4. Make a welcome speech to the government delegation from Australia.

4 Read the following dialogue and answer the questions.

G: Li Yang   L: Tour leader   T: A tourist

Li Yang is a tour guide in China International Travel Service. She is taking the tour group to the hotel. John Smith is the tour leader. Mr. Wang is the bus driver.

G: (To the tour leader) Excuse me, is everybody on the bus?
L: Yes, that's right.
G: Shall we go now?
L: Yeah, let's go.
G: (To all the guests on the tour bus) Ladies and gentlemen, now we are going straight to the hotel, the famous Beijing Hotel.

L: Where is the hotel located and how long can we get there?

G: Beijing Hotel is located at the entrance of Wangfujing Avenue, just 200 meters east of Tiananmen Square. It will take us no more than 40 minutes to get there.

L: Oh, thank you, Miss Li. And what time is it now?

G: It is 17:10, Beijing time, the time difference between Beijing and New York is 13 hours, please adjust your time forward for 13 hours.

L: Thank you, Miss Li.

G: It's my pleasure. Oh, by the way, I'd like to inform you today's weather. According the weather forecast, it's a fine day today and the highest temperature is 23 degree centigrade.

L: A nice day. Wonderful!

G: As we travel along, you'll have a view of the suburb and the city. Beijing has a long history. It has been an inhabited city for more than three thousand years. For more than 800 years, Beijing was a capital city—from the Yuan Dynasty (1271—1368) to the Ming (1368—1644) and Qing (1644—1911) dynasties. Thirty-four emperors have lived and ruled the nation in Beijing and it has been an important trading city from its earliest days. Beijing, located in the northeast of China and surrounded by Hebei Province, covers an area of 16,800 square kilometers. This is very much a flat city. The city has four distinctively recognizable seasons. Basically, autumn and May are the best time to visit Beijing. You are very lucky to come here in this May. The present city has a population of over 13.8 million. Beijing is the capital of China. It is the center of China's political, cultural and international activities. All kinds of culture festivals and international symposiums are held in Beijing every year. Just as you know, the 29th Olympic Games has been hosted successfully in Beijing this year. There is no doubt that Beijing shows its new image of an open, modern and well-developed metropolis to the rest of the world. Oh, my dear friends, will you come to China again?

T: Yes, we will.

G: Thank you. If possible, I'd also like to be your guide. Beijing is an ancient city with a history of more than 690,000 years. Chinese history has strewn the land of Beijing with sites of cultural and historical interest. Some of them, such as Tiananmen Square, the Great Wall, the Forbidden City, the Temple of Heaven, the Summer Palace, and the ruins of Peking Man at Zhoukoudian, are world cultural heritage sites.

T: Where is the Forbidden City? I'm looking forward to visiting it.

G: The famous Forbidden City is in the centre of the city. Tomorrow morning we'll pay a visit to Tiananmen Square and the Forbidden City.

T: That's great.

G: Furthermore, you can touch the local culture and lifestyle. There is a popular saying, which goes, "No dining experience is complete without sampling the delicious delicacy of Peking Roast Duck." Personally, I think you should have a taste of it. Then you can go to the theatre to enjoy Peking Opera and Acrobatic Show at night. They are really very amazing. Look, can you see that beautiful building? It is the Beijing Hotel. Here we are at the hotel.

■ **Key points for an enroute guiding.**

1. Inform the tourists of the itinerary briefly.
2. Comment on the enroute scenery.
3. Make a brief introduction to the city (including its location, area, population, history, climate, life, culture and customs, etc.).
4. If time permitted, organize entertainment activities to promote the friendship and atmosphere between the guide and the tourists.

VOCABULARY ASSISTANT

distinctively 区别地   recognizable 可辨认的
symposium 讨论会   metropolis 大都会

1. Where is the Beijing Hotel located?

2. What's the time difference between Beijing and New York?

3. According the weather forecast, what's the weather like in Beijing?

4. How many dynasties' capitals were in Beijing? What are they?

5. What's the best time for the tourists to visit Beijing?

6. How many emperors lived and ruled their countries in Beijing?

7. Which Olympic Games was held in Beijing?

8. Please list the famous scenic spots in Beijing as many as you know.

9. What's the population in Beijing?

10. What's the most delicious food in Beijing.

5 **Try to fill in the following chart about how to make an enroute guiding.**

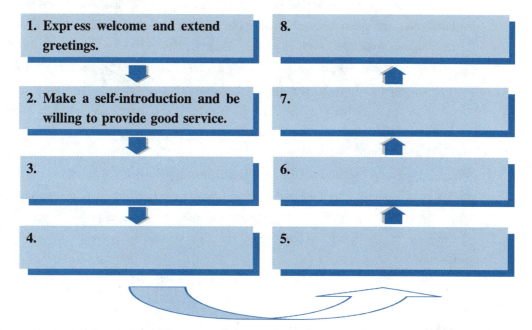

1. Express welcome and extend greetings.
2. Make a self-introduction and be willing to provide good service.
3.
4.
5.
6.
7.
8.

6 **Rewrite the following passage into a dialogue and practice with your partners.**

> Good morning, everybody. Now I'd like make a brief introduction to Hebei Province.
>
> Hebei Province has a long history. It's abbreviation is "Ji." In the Spring and Autumn period, its north part belonged to Yan State and its south was in Zhao State. So, it got its nickname "Yanzhao." It has been called Hebei since 1928.
>
> It is located in the North China Plain, on the north bank of the Yellow River, west of Bohai Bay. The exact location is from 113.04 degrees to 119.53 degrees longitude in the east, and from 36.01 degrees to 42.37 degrees latitude in the north. It covers an area of 187,700 square kilometers, with Taihang Mountain in its west and Yashan Mountain in its north. The north part of Yanshan Mountain is the Zhangbei Plateau, other parts are called Hebei Plain. The highest point of Hebei province is called Small Wutai, which is 2,870 meters in elevation, and the elevation of about 43% is no more than 100 meters.

The weather here is moderate. It is said that it encounters monson season, so the four seasons are obvious. It is cold and with little snow in winter while hot and much rainfall in summer, windy in short spring and cool in autumn. The average temperature is from −27 to 2 degrees centigrade in January and from 18 to 27 in July. The annual precipitation is from 350 to 750 millimeter approximately.

For the purpose of administration, Hebei Province is divided into 11 cities, 109 counties and six autonomous counties. The capital city is Shijiazhuang. There are many ethnic nationalities, such as Uygur, Manchu, Mongolian and Korean etc.

There are many scenic spots and relics in Hebei Province. Chengde and Baoding have been listed into the "Historical and Cultural cities in China". Many parts of the Great Wall are in Hebei province. There are many scenic spots and religious relics, such as the largest imperial garden-the Mountain Resort and its Outlying Temples, the splendid Eastern and Western Qing Tombs, the Han Tomb Complex, Zhaozhou Bridge, Longxing Temple and the Iron Lion. Among them, the Mountain Resort and its Outlying Temples and the Eastern Qing Tombs have been listed to the world cultural heritage by the UNESCO. For the natural resources, Beidaihe in Qinhuangdao are famous for seashore, and the Mulan Hunging Ground is well-known for its vast grassland.

7 **Cultural Salon: Read the following passage, try to get some cultural knowledge about *Chinese Local Customs* and answer the questions.**

There are many habits and customs that are particular to China and Chinese people.

Chinese names are given in the reverse of Western names. The surname is said first, and then the given name. Professional, social, and family tittles always follow the name as well. The titles Doctor, Master, Professor, or Teacher would follow the surname or full name.

Unlike Westerners, Chinese people do not usually greet people who they have not been introduced to or are not familiar with. It would seem odd if a person would offer a "Hi" or "Hello" when passing on the street. Chinese people often greet friends or acquaintances by asking whether they have eaten or by asking where they are going. It is also standard practice to have a name card or business card to give to people when introduced.

Rice or noodles are served with virtually every meal. For breakfast, Chinese people generally eat congee (over-boiled rice), dumplings, or noodles. At lunch a Chinese person generally eats a single rice or noodle dish themselves. In some areas boxes of rice with vegetables, pork, chicken, etc. are very popular. Dinner is a family affair. In Chinese dinners, all the dishes are placed on a center table. Each person is given a bowl of soup. After the soup is finished, the bowl is filled with rice and everyone takes what they want from the dishes on the table.

Chinese people are big on treating people to dinner. It is common for a person to take a friend to dinner or lunch, just as in many Western cultures. Chinese people often vie to be the one to pay the bill. Chinese people also invite other people or families to their residence to eat quite often. When one is invited to a person's residence they should eat all the rice in a bowl and eat some of each dish.

In China drinking tea has a long history of 4,000 years. It has become a special phenomenon and it is an indispensable beverage in daily lives of Chinese people. You can see teahouses scattered on street similar to the ways that coffeehouses are often seen in the West. Although there are hundreds of varieties of Chinese tea, they can be mainly classified into five categories, which are, green tea, black tea, brick tea, scented tea, and Oolong tea. Chinese people are very critical about tea. They have high requirements about tea quality, and tea ware.

In China, there are customs about tea. A host will inject tea into teacup only seven tenth, and it is said the other three tenth will be filled with friendship and affection. Moreover, the teacup should be empty in three gulps. Tea plays an important role in Chinese emotional life. Serving a cup of tea is more than a matter of mere politeness, it is a symbol of togetherness. It signifies respect and the sharing of something enjoyable with visitors.

In Chinese culture, color has a special significance. The color red is one of good luck and prosperity. Gold is the imperial color. White is the color of death (and is the color traditionally worn at funerals). Black symbolizes misfortune.

Chinese like hilarity. On festivals, it is happier and everywhere is full of exciting air. Though in the freedom Chinese washed and globed by the western culture, every traditional entertainment of the festivals have not stopped and vanished. Many folk custom and entertainments have handed down from generation to generation.

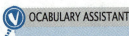

indispensable 不可缺少的　　　　　　**signify** 表示
emotional 情感的　　　　　　　　　　**hilarity** 热闹

1. What is the difference between Chinese names and Western names?
_____

2. How do Chinese people greet friends or acquaintances?
_____

3. What will Chinese people eat for breakfast?
_____

4. Could you tell us some names of Chinese tea?
_____

5. Why do Chinese people like drinking tea?
_____

Further reading: What do others see when they look at you?

  A mirror reflects your appearance exactly as it is. Your reflection in a mirror is exactly how you appear to a customer. First expressions are very important. The first thing a customer sees is your clothing, grooming, and facial expression.

  Your clothing should be suitable for the situation. Your grooming is also important. Fragrances, hairstyle, and makeup should be appropriate. At the normal distance between you and a customer, the customer cannot only see and hear you, but can smell you. A ready smile is an important contributor to your outward appearance. Remember, your customers are watching you when you watch their facial expression.

  After seeing you, your customer will hear your voice. In some cases this may occur at the same time. A good speaking voice and speech habits will enhance your presentation. A good voice should be warm and friendly. Lower voice tones generally sound warmer than high tones. Although you can not change your voice, you can control your volume pitch, and articulation. Don't talk too fast or too slow.

Certain speech habits can also become obstacle. Mumbling, mispronouncing, and using slang can be irritating to your customers. A simple way to discover whether you suffer from any voice or speech problems is to record your voice. Many people are surprised to hear how they sound.

Many people have little habits that are annoying to others. You can probably think of a friend or acquaintance that has a habit that is annoying. Continuously taping your fingers on a table top, removing and replacing glasses, or playing with a pen or pencil are examples of mannerisms that may find annoying. Be conscious of your behavior patterns. Ask your family and friends if you have consistent, noticeable mannerisms that may bother them. Once discovered, make a real effort to correct them.

Good manners will enhance your image in the eyes of your customer. Simple things such as offering a friendly "Good morning", or "Have a nice day", will make your customer feel good and don't cost you anything.

Certain personality traits are helpful to a successful service career. These traits should be cultivated. Empathy is the ability to see things through the eyes of others, to put you in someone else's shoes. The more clearly you understand the feelings, need, problems of your customers, the better you can satisfy them. Empathy is closely related to interest. An interested tour guide constantly thinks in terms of customers' benefits. Customers will appreciate your interest and will respond accordingly.

Proper respect should be shown to all customers. Your respect shows your appreciation and judgment. Your customers will notice this and show a greater appreciation for you.

A smile and friendly attitude are contagious. A cheerful smile and greeting will help to put your customers in a good mood. Furthermore, your cheerful attitude will improve your outlook, so that when problems are encountered, they will seem less formidable. A cheerful person is not one who has solved every problem, but is one who unafraid to face problems and solve them. Your optimism will spread to those around you. Always leave your troubles at home or in the office. Never burden your customers with your problems.

Self-confidence is a belief in yourself that makes others believe in you. Self-confidence grows with experience. When you have tried and succeeded, you develop a confidence. You will have a feeling of knowing what to do and when to do it. How do you develop self-confidence if you don't have it? Start each day with a positive attitude. Before each tour, tell yourself that you know you can do well. Set little goals for yourself. As you achieve each goal, your self-confidence will grow. As your belief in yourself and your abilities grows, set higher goals. With enough self-confidence, you will be amazed at what you can achieve.

8 **Work in Pairs.**

> **Student A** A tourist from Britain.
>
> **Student B** A local tour guide.
> Student B introduces some Chinese local customs to Student A.

9 **Supplementary task: Make a welcome speech in class within ten minutes and then give an enroute guiding from Beijing Airport to Beijing Hotel. The teacher and students will remark on your performance.**

Unit 3 Arriving at the Hotel

AIMS

- To know how many room types there are in a hotel
- To understand how to make a check-in
- To learn the service procedure of the front desk
- To master the basic words and expressions of check-in and check-out
- To remember what to remind the guests when check out

START-UP

Make a list of all the room types you know in a hotel.

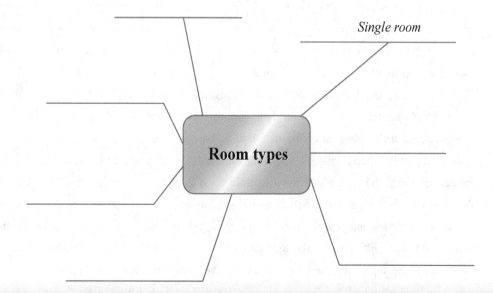

1 Read the following passage and answer the questions.

Check-in

The tourists are from abroad, they can be divided into two kinds—the individual guests and the group guests. Individual guests means that guests are no more than ten, there are no tour leader in the group; while group guests means that the number of the group is more than ten, as usual, there must be a tour leader in the group to take care of the guests. So the service procedures to the two kinds of people are different.

While showing the individual guests to the hotel, the tour guide must remind them to get their passports ready, and he must tell some specific information of the guests to the front desk, such as the number of the guests, the number of the rooms, the name of the travel agency, the name of the person who reserves the rooms... etc., in order to avoid of making mistakes. Because the guests may have difficulties in communicating, the tour guide should try his best to offer the best service to the guests, he should explain all kinds of possibility to help the guests to check in. Therefore, the tour guide must be quite familiar with the room types. As usual, there are single rooms, twin rooms, double rooms, suites, deluxe suites, studio rooms, and duplexes. The tour guide must make sure about the room types the guests need and help the guests with the formalities. The guests should show their passports to the front desk, sometimes, the clerk of the front desk will fill in the registration form with the information shown on the passports, sometimes, the hotel will ask the guests to fill in the form by themselves, at this time, the tour guide should help the guests who have difficulties, so the tour guide must be quite familiar with the registration form, usually, the following information must be included although different hotels have different forms, they are: surname (family name), given name (first name), sex, age, date of birth, place of birth, nationality, passport number, reason of stay, arrival date, departure date, type of visa and signature. If the guests have difficulties in understanding, the tour guide must explain each item to them. After finishing all the formalities, the guests can get their room keys, as an experienced tour guide, he must make every arrangement well in order not to bother the guests later, so before letting the guests go to their rooms, the tour guide must tell them the location of the elevator, the time to get together, the place to get together and other necessary information.

The procedure of helping group guests check in is a little different from that of individual guests. As usual, there will be a tour leader in the group, and he will have a group visa, and the necessary information of the guests is shown on it, so it's unnecessary for the guests to show their passports at the hotel. The tour guide should communicate with the clerk at the front desk first and make sure he can get the right rooms, then, he should ask the tour leader to show his group visa to the front desk, and the clerk at the front desk will make a copy of it. After that, the tour guide should help the tour leader distribute the rooms, certainly, before showing the room keys to the guests, the guide should remind them of the necessary information of the rest arrangement.

VOCABULARY ASSISTANT

the individual guests 散客   distribute 分配,分给
the group guests 团队客人   formality 手续

1. Do you know the difference between individual guests and group guests?
_____

2. How does a tour guide help the individual guests to check in?
_____

3. What information should the tourists fill in to complete the registration form?
_____

4. Before letting the guests go to their rooms, what should an experienced tour guide do?
_____

5. Do the group tourists need to show their passport?
_____

2 Fill in the gaps with a suitable word from the box. Change their forms if necessary.

| room type | reservation | registration form | bother | individual guest |
| group guest | formality | tour leader | distribute | best service |

1. While showing the _____ to the hotel, the tour guide must remind them to get their passports ready.

2. The tour guide should try his best to offer the _____ to the guests.

3. I'm John Smith., the tour guide of a group. We made a _____ through the Travel Service yesterday.

4. The tour guide must make sure about the room types the guests need and help the guests with the _____.

5. Please fill in the _____.

6. The tour guide must be quite familiar with the _____.

7. As an experienced tour guide, he must make every arrangement well in order not to _____ the guests later.
8. The procedure of helping _____ check in is a little different from that of individual guests.
9. As usual, there will be a _____ in the group.
10. The tour guide should help the tour leader _____ the rooms.

3 **Talk about the following pictures and distinguish them correctly.**

A twin room

A double room

Checking in for individual guests

Checking in for group guests

4 **Read the following passage and answer the questions.**

Check-out

After the whole visiting in one place, the tourists will leave for another destination, before that, the tour guide must remind the guests of many aspects in order to help them to finish the formalities at the front desk.

While going sightseeing, the tourists from abroad must have a lot of luggage, when travel from one place to another, they may have many chances to change the hotels, so they must pack up their luggage before leaving, under this circumstances, the tour guide must tell the tourists about the time arrangement one day earlier, and leave enough time for them to collect luggage. Usually, the bellman of the hotel can help the tourists to take down the big luggage, but it must be arranged by the tour guide since there are so many tourist groups in one hotel, if the group will leave early on next morning, he should remind the tourists to pack up their luggage well and leave them out of their rooms at certain time, in this way, the bellman can collect all of them together, and the luggage won't be lost. If the group will check out early on next morning, the guide should arrange a wake-up call for the tourists, he should tell both the clerk at the front desk and the tourists, in order to avoid of being late for other activities.

As usual, in early morning, the front desk must be very busy, because here is a regulation in all the hotels all over China, that is, the guest must check out before 12:00, or they will be surcharged. In order to save time, the guide should tell the tourists to pay for their long-distance call in advance, if the tourists have consumed something in the room or the hotel, they'd better pay for it in advance too.

Besides the above-mentioned information, the guide should remind the tourists to return their room keys at certain time, usually, the time should be ten to fifteen minutes earlier than the set-off time.

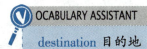

OCABULARY ASSISTANT

destination 目的地   regulation 规律   surcharge 额外收费

1. What should you remind the guests before they check out?

2. Is it necessary to arrange a wake-up call for the guests if they will check out early on next morning?

3. Who can help the tourists to take down the big luggage?

4. As usual, in early morning, the front desk must be very busy, why?

5. When should the guest check out? Or they will be surcharged.

6. Which do you think is the first thing guests should do before leaving?

7. How to comfort and help the guest when the bellmen deliver bags to the wrong room?

8. What would you do if there were any mistakes in your bill?

9. Who should pay for the extra costs in a hotel?

10. Who plays the main role in making a check-in or check-out, the tour guide or the tour leader?

5 Try to fill in the following chart about how to check in.

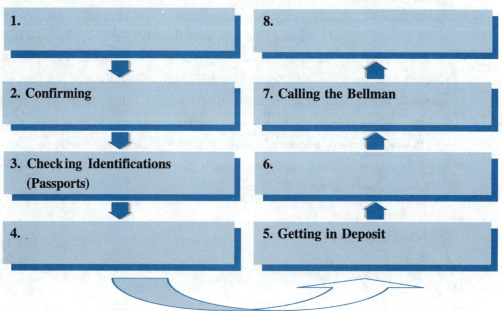

1.	8.
2. Confirming	7. Calling the Bellman
3. Checking Identifications (Passports)	6.
4.	5. Getting in Deposit

6 Rewrite the dialogue and practice with your partners.

Checking Out for a Group

C: Cashier   G: Tour Guide

G: (In the evening) How time flies! We'll check out tomorrow morning, our departure time is at 9 a.m. Would you be here by 8:50 a.m. at latest? Could you place your bags in front of your room by 8:00 tomorrow morning? The bellman will collect them.
(The next morning)

G: Is everybody here? (Counting the guests) yes, everyone is here.

G: Then let us collect the room keys and check out.

C: Good morning, sir, Can I help you?

G: I'd like to pay our hotel bill now. My name is Harry Carpenter, I am the tour guide of the group.

C: Just a moment please, Mr. Carpenter... Sorry to have kept you waiting. Here's your bill. The total is RMB8,050 Yuan, including 15 percent surcharge.

G: I think RMB8,000 is reasonable! What's that RMB50 for? Is there a mistake?

C: Please examine the bill carefully and I'll explain it for you.

G: Of course, I'll check it.

C: One of your guests drank two bottles of beer in the room. And the price of each is RMB25. So you have altogether RMB50 extra charge.

G: Ok. I see. Thank you for the explanation.

C: You are welcome, sir. We hope you have enjoyed your stay in the hotel.

G: (Turn to the guests) Good morning, ladies and gentlemen. We're checking out. Who drank the beer in the room yesterday? Could you please pay your incidental charges at the Front Cashier's Desk?

G: Ok, we'll get on the coach now. Please don't leave your belongings at the hotel.

OCABULARY ASSISTANT

departure 离开   incidental charges 额外费用(如客人自己在酒店的消费)

7 Cultural Salon: Read the following passage, try to get some cultural knowledge about *Chinese Cuisine* and answer the questions.

As we know, China is famous for many things in the world, and one of them is Chinese Cuisine. There are so many kinds of cuisine in China, typically, we have "Four Cuisines", they are Sichuan Cuisine, Shandong Cuisine, Guangdong Cuisine (Cantonese) and Zhejiang-Jiangsu Cuisine. Different cuisine has its unique feature, special flavor and famous dishes.

Sichuan cuisine is hot and tongue-numbing, the typical dishes are: twice-cooked pork slices[1], spicy diced chicken with peanuts[2], dry-fried shark fin[3], fish-flavored pork shreds[4] and pork-marked woman's bean curd[5]; Shandong cuisine is fresh, tasty but now greasy, the typical dishes are: yellow river carp in sweet and sour sauce[6], stewed/agate sea cucumber[7], Dezhou braised chicken[8], Beijing roast duck, shrimps wearing jade belts[9], eight immortals crossing the sea[10]; Guangdong cuisine, also known as Cantonese in the world, is fresh, tender and light-seasoned, its typical dishes are: dragon and tiger locked in battle[11], roast snake with chrysanthemum blooms[12], roast suckling pig [13], duck web in oyster sauce [14], braised chicken feet with wild herbs[15]; Jiangsu-Zhejiang cuisine is sweet and sour, the cutting technique and the temperature control are emphasized, the typical dishes are: crystal pork[16], braised shark fin in brown sauce[17], simmered pork head[18], eel and crab meat in crab shells[19], west lake fish in vinegar sauce[20].

Chinese food is quite different from that of other countries, so while translating the names, the tour guide will meet a great challenge, as usual, the English name of Chinese dishes consists of four parts, and they are the raw material, the cutting way, the cooking way and the seasoning. Generally, the raw material can be divided into the following categories: chicken, duck, fish, pork, seafood, game, eggs, vegetables, soybean products, dairy products, fruits and nuts. The cutting way, or the shape of the material is like slices, strips, shreds, cubes, segments, grains and mince. The cooking technique includes quick-frying, stir-frying, roasting, sautéing, simmering, braising, smoking, steaming and stewing; Seasoning usually consists of salty, sweet, sour, pungent flavors (spicy, hot, tongue-numbing etc.).

VOCABULARY ASSISTANT

greasy 油腻的   emphasize 强调   shred 细条
cube 立方体   segment 段   grain 粒状物
sauté 炒, 嫩煎 simmer 炖   pungent 刺鼻; 辛辣的
tongue-numbing 舌头麻木的

NOTES

[1] 回锅肉   [2] 宫保鸡丁   [3] 干烧鱼翅   [4] 鱼香肉丝
[5] 麻婆豆腐 [6] 糖醋鲤鱼   [7] 玛瑙海参   [8] 德州扒鸡
[9] 玉带虾仁 [10] 八仙过海 [11] 龙虎斗   [12] 菊花烤蛇
[13] 烤乳猪   [14] 蚝油鸭蹼 [15] 药膳鸡爪 [16] 水晶猪肉
[17] 浇汁鱼翅 [18] 炖猪头   [19] 元壳膳蟹 [20] 西湖醋鱼

1. How many famous cuisines are there in China?

2. What are the different features?

3. Try to tell the typical dishes of "Four Cuisines"?

4. What are the raw materials we generally use in Chinese cooking?

5. Speak out at least five kinds of cooking technique?

Further reading: Chinese Cuisine

Chinese food, rich and colorful, has, as its main features: various color, aromatic flavor, and excellent taste. With these three characteristics, Chinese cuisine is not only tasty but also a work of art for people to appreciate. To make real Chinese food, none of the three characteristics: color, aroma and delicious taste should be excluded.

Various Colors

Food with beautiful color can usually greatly arouse people's appetite. For many years, Chinese food preparation has paid attention to artistic appearance. To have a bright, pleased and harmonious color is one of the main principles when cooking Chinese food. To achieve this, add two or three ingredients with different colors are added as decoration to complement the main ingredient. Thus, it is not only the taste of Chinese cuisine that makes you amazed but also its artistic value.

Aromatic Flavor

Chinese people attach great importance to the aroma of the dish. Usually aniseed, Chinese prickly ash seeds, cinnamon and other spices are added to help dispel the ingredients' particular smells, such as foul, fishy and mutton smells. Also some other flavors like shallot, ginger, garlic or chili, cooking wine and sesame oil are added to make the food fragrant in flavor.

Excellent Taste

Regarded as the soul of the Chinese dish, taste can be divided into five classes: sweet, sour, bitter, hot and salty. Seasoning such as soy sauce, sugar, vinegar and salt in proper amount and in different sequences, contribute to the taste of the dish. In the vast land of China, there are eating habits of "South-Sweet, North-Salty, East-Hot and West-Sour" according to the different tastes of the people. Those in southern China like to add more sugar when cooking than others. Jiangsu Cuisine is representative of "South-Sweet." Shandong Cuisine feature more salt and people living in Hunan, Hubei, Jiangxi, Guizhou, and Sichuan like chili best. Sour flavor is favored by Shanxi, Fujian, Guangxi people and the northeasterners.

When a banquet is held, usually ten to twelve people sit around a table to enjoy the bounteous feast. Delicious hot and cold dishes with different tastes and flavors cooked in different ways are served. Together with the various colors of the dishes, everyone can't help marveling at the rich Chinese dietetic culture.

8 **Work in Pairs.**

> **Student A** You are the tour guide.
>
> **Student B** You are the guest who is a vegetarian, you don't want garlic.
> Student A offers help to arrange special dishes for Student B.

9 **Supplementary task: Give a brief introduction to one of Chinese dishes you know. Maybe it is from your hometown, or it is your favorite. Make a presentation in five minutes in class. The teacher and students will make comments on what you tell and how the presentation can be improved.**

Unit 4

Talking about Tour Arrangement

AIMS

- To understand what and how to prepare for talking about a tour itinerary
- To find ways to improve your guiding skills and performance
- To master the basic words and expressions of talking about tour arrangement
- To know the basic elements of the tour itinerary such as transportation, accommodation, entrance ticket, guide service, destination

START-UP

Make a list of all the common words you know for talking about tour arrangement.

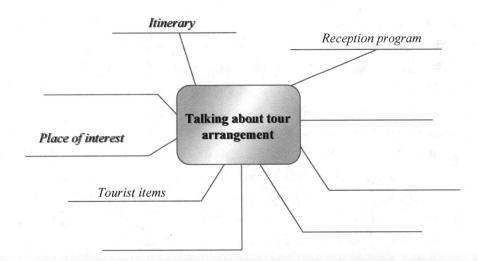

UNIT 4 TALKING ABOUT TOUR ARRANGEMENT

1 Read the following conversation and answer the questions.

Discussing the Itinerary

L: Local guide   N: National guide   T: Tour leader

(*In the hotel lobby, Liu Mei, the local guide from Beijing International Travel Service, is going to discuss the itinerary with the tour leader Ms White and the national guide Mr. Lee*)

L: Excuse me, Ms White, Mr. Lee; I'd like to discuss the itinerary for our trip with you.

N: Sure. Ms White, Is it convenient for you right now?

T: Certainly. Let's go over our tour itinerary now. I got a copy of the itinerary of this trip from my travel service before I left for China. Can we do as our scheduled?

L: Yes, we can. If you want to make any changes, minor alternations can be made then.

T: That's fine.

N: Well, our trip includes four days sightseeing in Beijing and threes days sightseeing in Xian, and then we will visit the Mountain Resort of Chengde and Lama Temples for two more days sightseeing. Liu Mei will give us a detailed introduction to the tour itinerary of Beijing, will you?

L: Oh, yes, it is part of my job as the local guide of Beijing. I'm afraid that you'll be exhausted after long flight. The rest of this afternoon is free at your own leisure. Dinner is arranged in the restaurant of this hotel at 6:00 p.m.

T: We are quite ok now. Everyone in this group is eager to visit Beijing. Can we possibly see something of Beijing after dinner?

N: How about Peking Opera?

L: We will enjoy a Peking Opera tomorrow evening according to the schedule. What do you think about acrobatics? This is an option, if we arrange this program for our tourists; they should pay 60 Yuan for the show. Perhaps this will interest you.

T: It sounds marvelous! I'll inform them before dinner. Let's play that by ear.

L: We will first visit the historic Tiananmen Square, the largest city square in the world and the spiritual heart of China, where the national flag is raised exactly at sunrise everyday, and then the Forbidden City tomorrow morning. In the afternoon, we will visit splendid Temple of Heaven. We will enjoy a Peking Opera in the evening.

T: How long will the show last?

L: The show will take about an hour and a half. We ought to be back here by 9:00 p.m.

Next day we will visit the majestic Great Wall in the morning, the Ding Tomb of the Ming Dynasty and the Sacred Road in the afternoon. And we will enjoy the famous Peking Roast Duck for dinner.

T: Shall we come back to hotel for a short rest before dinner? I know someone in this group is willing to take a bath before big banquet, and we get used to eating around 7:30 p.m. for dinner.

L: I'm afraid that I must say sorry. We can not waste our valuable time on the way. On the fourth day, after breakfast, we will visit the Summer Palace, the best-preserved royal garden in China with a history of over 800 years. We will visit Hutongs by rickshaw after the garden. Lunch will be served in one of the local people's home during the tour, where you can learn how to make dumplings. And then we will visit the Yonghe Lamasery and Beihai Park.

T: I wonder if it is possible to arrange shopping for us.

N: You can shop in Xiushui Street Market after the visiting of Beihai Park, where you can find traditional Chinese handicrafts, silk products, pearls, chinaware, traditional Chinese brand products, etc.

L: Well, eating Peking Roast Duck and shopping at Xiushui Street have become a must for foreign visitors to Beijing.

T: It's wonderful. Thanks for everything you've done for us!

L: My pleasure. I really wish you'll have a pleasant stay here.

T: This is our common desire.

L: I'm afraid that I'll go and inform the morning call for our group, see you at 6:00 in the lobby.

N: Good-bye. Have a nice day!

T: Thanks. See you.

OCABULARY ASSISTANT

scheduled 预定的
option 选项,选择权,[经]买卖的特权
majestic 宏伟的,庄严的
exhausted 耗尽的,疲惫的
Let's play that by ear. 视情况而定。
sacred 神的,宗教的,庄严的,神圣的

1. What special attention should be paid to in discussing the tour itinerary as a local tour guide?

2. Suppose you are a national tour guide, what will you do if the tour leader wants to cancel some programs during the tour?

3. What have you learnt about itinerary planned from this dialogue?
_____

4. What kind of view can we enjoy in Tiananmen Square?
_____

5. Is it a must to eat Peking Roast Duck during your visit in Beijing?
_____

2 Fill in the gaps with a suitable word from the box. Change their forms if necessary.

take	rest	detail	pleasant	preserve
according to	majestic	afraid	be eager to	serve

1. She will give us a _____ introduction to the tour itinerary of Beijing.
2. I really wish you'll have a _____ stay here.
3. The Summer Palace is the best _____ royal garden in China with a history of over 800 years.
4. The _____ of this afternoon is free at your own leisure.
5. Everyone in this group _____ visit Beijing.
6. We will enjoy a Peking Opera tomorrow evening _____ the schedule.
7. I'm _____ that I'll go and inform the morning call for our group.
8. Lunch will be _____ in one of the local people's home during the tour.
9. The show will _____ about an hour and a half.
10. We will visit the _____ Great Wall in the morning, the Ding Tomb of the Ming Dynasty and the Sacred Road in the afternoon.

3 Talk about the tour itinerary in pairs according to the map.

◯	Provincial Capital, Autonomous Region Municipality, Special Administrative Region
○	City Scenic Spot
▲	Mountain
☆	Capital
○ △ ☆	the Site on the ltinerany
⌒	Strike Line
✈	Start City and End City (If the start city and end city are the same, one only destination symbol is marked)

4 Please read the following dialogue and answer the questions.

Itinerary Planning

C: Clerk   T: Tourist

C: Good morning. China International Travel Service. May I help you?

T: Good morning. I want to inquire about a 9-day tour program to the north of China. Could you arrange a tour for us?

C: We've got several popular routes in the north. What kind of view do you prefer to visit?

T: I prefer scenic spots to historical interest. I do not care too much about what kind of view; I just want to relax myself. Which place do you recommend?

C: How about the tour of Beijing—Dalian—Shenyang—Harbin? You will visit the Imperial Palace of Shenyang; also you can enjoy the wonderful view of Mountain Qian by cable, which is the most famous mountain in north of China.

T: How about the view of Dalian and Harbin?

C: Dalian is a trading and financial center in northeastern Asia and has gained the name the "Hong Kong of Northern China", you will visit the Romantic Golden Pebble Beach. And then you will visit the Xinghai Square, Which looks like a star in the map. The itinerary of Harbin includes the Sun Island, where you can enjoy the fun of Ice Sculpture Art, Zhaolin Park Ice Lantern and so on.

T: Oh, it's wonderful. But I have been to Beijing before. Can you arrange another city for me?

C: What do you think about Changchun? Changchun is one of the important market-

> places and good distribution centers in the Northeast. You can visit Puppet Manchurian Palace, where is the last emperor's palace in China, then visit movie factory or car factory, which is the biggest in China.
>
> **T:** That sounds good. Do I travel on my own?
>
> **C:** No. This is a package tour. Our travel agency charters the plane or the bus, reserves accommodation in the four-star hotel and offers an English speaking guide and the entrance ticket of the scenic spots.
>
> **T:** How much does it cost per person?
>
> **C:** $365 per person for nine days, including four-star hotel accommodation, guide service, transportation between cities, local transportation, the entrance ticket, and the return airfare.
>
> **T:** Does the price contain the air ticket from Beijing to Manila?
>
> **C:** No. Here are some brochures about the tour and the service we offer.
>
> **T:** Thank you for your help! I'll be here later. See you.
>
> **C:** You are welcome. We are looking forward to serving you again. Good-Bye.

1. What's the definition of an itinerary in your opinion?

2. What should a local guide do in order to avoid any careless ambiguity for the itinerary?

3. What kinds of changes may often happen to the tour itinerary during a tour?

4. What will the tour guide do if the tourists want to prolong the visit?

5. Can you change a scheduled tour itinerary if some tourists ask you to go shopping?

6. What is the function of the tour itinerary?

7. If most tourists in your group want to visit an additional program, but still some one in your group wants to visit the scheduled program, what will you do as a local guide?

8. What element is the most important when you plan an itinerary for tourist? Why?

9. If a tour guide wants to develop a new itinerary, what should the guide do?

10. Write a tour itinerary of 15 days for tourists. Why do you design the itinerary like this?

5 **Try to fill in the following chart about the basic factors of planning the tour itinerary.**

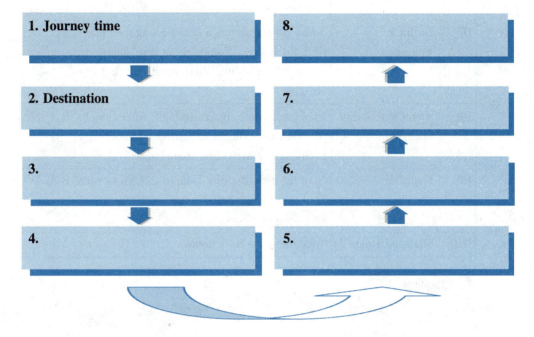

6 **Rewrite the scheduled itinerary into a dialogue and practice with your partners.**

China 10 days tour—Beijing, Xi'an, Guilin and Shanghai

Dates	Destinations	Activities	Meals Included
D1	Arrive in Beijing	Airport to Hotel Transfer (Beijing)	
D2	Beijing	Visit Tiananmen Square, the Forbidden City. After lunch, visit the Temple of Heaven.	B, L
D3	Beijing	Visit the Great Wall, Afternoon at leisure for shopping.	B, L, D
D4	Beijing to Xian	Take an early morning flight to Xi'an. Transfer to the Hotel, and then take a tour of the Big Wild Goose Pagoda and the Bell Tower. Enjoy a little free time in the afternoon.	B, L
D5	Xi'an	Visit to the Museum of Terra-cotta Warriors and Horses. After lunch, visit the Neolithic Village of Banpo which contains relics from the earliest known inhabitants of China.	B, L

D6	Xi'an to Guilin	Take a morning flight to Guilin. Upon arrival, begin sightseeing with a city tour, including Reed Flute Cave and Fubo Hill.	B,L
D7	Guilin to Yangshou	Today's excursion is a cruise along the beautiful Li River. Disembark at the charming village of Yangshuo, Visit Moon Hill and Big Banyan.	B,L
D8	Yangshuo-Guilin/Shanghai	Free at leisure in Yangshuo. After lunch, transfer to the Guilin airport for late afternoon to Shanghai. Arrival in Shanghai.	B,L,D
D9	Shanghai	Visit the Jade Buddha Temple and Yu Garden in the morning. After lunch, visit the Bund and Nanjing Road.	B,L,D
D10	Shanghai/Home	Take the plane back home.	AB

OCABULARY ASSISTANT

neolithic 新石器时期　　reed 芦苇　　flute 长笛　　banyan 榕树　　bund 码头

7　Cultural Salon: Read the following passage, try to get some cultural knowledge about *Chinese Literature* and answer the questions.

　　Ancient literature is a precious cultural heritage of China's several thousand years of civilization. The four masterpieces in Chinese classical literature enjoy good reputation and are widely spread among the readers. They are *Outlaws of the Marsh* by Shi Nai'an, *The Romance of the Three Kingdoms* by Luo Guanzhong, *Journey to the West* by Wu Cheng'en and *The Dream of Red Mansion* by Cao Xueqin and produced during the period of Ming and Qing dynasties. They have been celebrated for centuries for their special style and rich cultural and historical connotations.

Outlaws of the Marsh

Outlaws of the Marsh is one of the best known and best loved of the ancient Chinese novels which have come down through the ages. This novel describes political corruption, murder, love, and martial arts. If you haven't read it yet, give it a try. It will leave you wanting more!

The novel was written by Shi Nai'an, who was good at telling historical stories with vivid, exciting characters. Outlaws of the Marsh summarizes the historical reasons for the rebellion, as well as the events themselves. The tale describes how cruel government can drove the people to rebel and sings the praises of its heroes with great enthusiasm.

The novel is set in the final years of the Song Dynasty, from 1101 to 1125. It tells how one hundred and eight men and women get together on Liang Mountain, Shandong Province, and how they fought bravely against corrupt rulers.

Most events in the story are based on the facts. Some of the events actually happened and some of the people actually existed. Their brave deeds were praised by the common people and gradually became folk legends. One of these tales is the story of TIGER KILLER, which is very popular in China.

1. What are the styles of the four masterpieces of Chinese classical literature?

2. When did the four masterpieces of Chinese classical literature appear?

3. What element makes those four masterpieces of Chinese classical literature famous?

4. Which novel do you like most among the four masterpieces of Chinese classical literature? Why or why not?

5. Do you know other masterpieces in Chinese literature?

Further reading: Chinese Folklore

Chinese folklore has a long history, going back several thousand years. It is the body of expressive Chinese culture, including non-verbal art forms and customary practices of everyday life such as proverbs, tales, legends, jokes, music, dance... The definition most widely accepted by current scholars is "artistic communication in small groups," Chinese folklore have been modified with emperors ordering the burning of old books and the printing of new ones more in fitting in different dynasty.

Mythological tales is one of popular forms of Chinese folklore. It began in the Wei and Jin Dynasties (220—420), when various writers were interested in inventing stories about gods and ghosts by the influence of Taoism and Buddhism. Representative Chinese mythological tales include Chinese Valentine's Day, the Chinese dragon, The Jade Emperor, and the Five Emperors. Such mentioned ancient heroes and leaders are both historical figures according to legend and important characters in mythical stories.

In the early period of the Qing Dynasty there appeared a literary genre named Zhiguai which is an anthology of short mythical stories written in the classical style. Strange Stories from Happiness Studio by Pu Songling is one of the most famous representative masterpieces of this kind. For some time it was a most popular book, praised and liked by many people.

The Butterfly Lovers is one of the most popular love stories in China. The story was also called "Chinese Romeo and Juliet." It tells the legend of Chinese lovers who could not get married in their lifetime due to different family backgrounds and turned into a butterfly couple after their death.

The Chinese Valentine's Day is also related with a famous Chinese folklore—The Story of Cowherd and Weaver Girl. This beautiful tale has its origins in the Han Dynasty. It tells a sweet love between the 7th daughter of the Jade Emperor and an orphaned cowherd. The Emperor separated both of them by force. The 7th daughter was forced to move to the star called Vega and the cowherd moved to the star named Altair. They are allowed to meet only once a year on the 7th day of 7th lunar month. Therefore the Chinese Valentine's Day is celebrated on the 7th day of the 7th lunar month according to the Chinese calendar.

Tale of the White Snake and *Madame MengJiang* together with *The Butterfly Lovers* and *the Story of Cowherd and Weaver Girl* are the four major ancient Chinese legends.

9 Work in Pairs.

Student A You are a tourist to China.

Student B You are a tour guide.

Student A asks Student B to talk about *Outlaws of the Marsh*. Student B tells the story of TIGER KILLER and some Chinese folklore to Student A.

10 **Supplementary task: Design a tour itinerary and make a presentation within ten minutes in class. The teacher and students will make comments on your presentation and tell you how the presentation can be improved.**

Unit 5 City Tour and Ancient Capitals

AIMS

- To understand what and how to prepare for talking about a city or an ancient capital
- To find ways to improve your guiding skills and performance
- To master the basic words and expressions of talking about a city or an ancient capital
- To know the city's history, geography, scenery, local dishes, folk handicraft, special local products, economy and tourism

START-UP

Make a list of all the common words you know in introducing a city or an ancient capital.

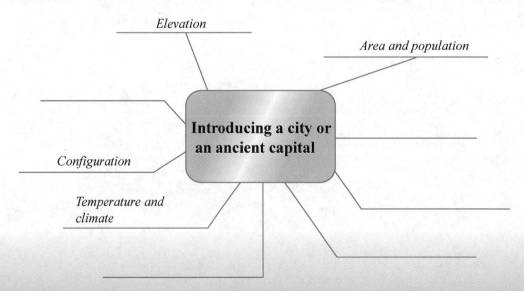

1 Read the following speech *Brief Introduction to Beijing* and answer the questions.

Ladies and Gentlemen,

Welcome to Beijing. Now we are leaving the Capital Airport for the hotel. Here, I'd like to give you a brief introduction about the Capital of China—Beijing.

Beijing is located in the northeast of China and surrounded by mountains to the east, west and north, with Yongding River flowing through the southwestern part. The total area is over 16,800 square kilometers and the total population is about 17 million people, among them, the mobile population is about 5.1 million dwelling in the capital. The climate here is a semi-humid, continental climate with an average temperature of 12℃ all year around.

As the capital of the People's Republic of China, Beijing is the nation's political, economic, cultural and educational center as well as being the most important center in China for international trade and communications. It has been the heart and soul of politics and society throughout its long history. Because of its role in the life and growth of China, there is an unequalled wealth available for travelers to discover as you experience Beijing's ancient past and enjoy its exciting 21st Century world. In August, 2008 Beijing hosted the Olympic Games, which has already showed the world something so special that everyone has been awestruck by Beijing's latest accomplishments, such as the famous Olympic stadiums—Bird's Nest and Water Cube, and the National Grand Theater, in the same time they have become not only the typical monuments of modern Beijing, but also the typical of China.

There are a lot of well-known sceneries in Beijing. The magnificent Forbidden City is the world's largest and best-preserved imperial palace complex. The Great Wall is one of the eight wonders of the world and is the only man-made structure that is visible from outer space with naked eyes by US Astronaut Neil Armstrong.

Beijing has many beautiful and fascinating temples, such as Temple of Heaven, Yonghe Lamasery. Temple of Heaven is the largest group of structures in the country dedicated to rituals that pay homage to heaven. The White Cloud Taoist Temple is one of the oldest and still the most active of Taoist temples in Beijing.

Tiananmen Square, the largest city central square in the world, solemn and respectful, is not only the symbol of Beijing, but also the symbol of China. Many historic events happened here. The square is surrounded by a variety of significant edifices: Chinese Revolution History Museum, Chairman Mao's Mausoleum, Great Hall of the People, the elegant and beautiful Tiananmen, which is also called Heavenly Peace Gate. The daily flag ceremony at the square, performed at sunrise and sunset every day, is most magnificent and well-worth making time to watch. Other famous attractions in Beijing include the Ming Tombs, the burial site of 13 ancient emperors; the Drum Tower built in the 1400's; Fragrant Hills Park and so on.

Why does the city have so many phenomenal places? If you get to know Beijing's history, you can find the answer. Beijing's long and illustrious history starts approximately 500,000 years ago. It is here that Peking men, the ancestors of modern Homo sapiens, lived in caves. Records show that Beijing has been an inhabited city for more than three thousand years and has lived through invasions, devastating fires, dynasties, warlords, Anglo-French troops and has emerged each time as a strong and vibrant city. For more than 800 years, Beijing was a capital city from the Yuan Dynasty to the Ming and Qing dynasties. Thirty-four emperors have lived and ruled in Beijing and it has been an important trading city from earliest days. Although now Beijing is modern, fashionable and full of 21st Century vitality, you can experience authentic Beijing life and become acquainted with "old Beijing" by visiting many tea houses, temple fares, Beijing's Hutong and Courtyard, enjoying the Peking Opera, tasting Beijing Roast Duck and other local dishes.

Now the beautiful Beijing is opening its arms to welcome friends from all over the world. Visiting Beijing, you will never be disappointed.

VOCABULARY ASSISTANT

semi-humid 半湿热　　continental 大陆性的　　awestruck 敬畏的
complex 综合建筑　　fascinating 很有吸引力　　phenomenal 非凡的
devastating 令人震惊的

1. As a tour guide when is it suitable to introduce a city and how to introduce?

2. If you are a local tour guide, which do you think is the most important during introducing a city?

3. According to your understanding, what tasks should a tour guide perform when foreign guests come to your city?

4. There are a lot of well-known sceneries in Beijing, old and new, please list some of them.

5. Why does the city have so many phenomenal places?

2 Fill in the gaps with a suitable word from the box. Change their forms if necessary.

Yuan Dynasty	semi-humid and continental	population	communications
economic	Ming and Qing Dynasties	thirty-four	locate
cover	ancestor		

1. Beijing is _____ in the northeast of China.
2. Beijing's climate is a _____ climate with an average temperature of 12℃.
3. It has a _____ of 17 million people.
4. Beijing _____ a total area of more than 16,800 square kilometers.
5. Beijing was a capital city from the _____ to the _____.
6. _____ emperors have lived and ruled in Beijing.
7. Beijing is the nation's political, _____, cultural and educational center as well as being the most important center in China for international trade and _____.
8. It is here that Peking men, the _____ of modern Homo sapiens, lived in caves.

3 Talk about the famous scenic spots in Beijing.

The Great Wall

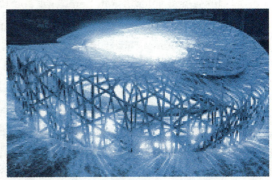

Bird's Nest

Temple of Heaven

Tiananmen Square

4 **Read the following passage and answer the questions.**

The Palace Museum

Now we are in the front of the Palace Museum. I'd like to show you around the Palace Museum. Follow me, please.

The Palace Museum, also known as the Forbidden City, was the imperial palaces for 24 emperors during the Ming and Qing dynasties. In early 15th century, the large-scale complex involved 100,000 artisans and one million workmen, took 14 years and was finished in 1420. In the following, the capital of the Ming Dynasty was moved from Nanjing to Beijing. Until 1925 the complex was converted into a museum. Since then the palace has been opened to the public. It is the best preserved and the largest ancient imperial palace in the world.

It is located in the center of Beijing. The Forbidden City consists of 9,999.5 rooms, rectangular in shape and 72 hectares in size, is surrounded by 10-meter high city wall and a 52-meter wide moat. At each corner of the wall stands a watchtower with a double-eave roof covered with yellow glazed tiles. It is indeed a city within a city.

Most of the structures are wooden, with white stone foundations, yellow glazed tiles, and colorful wall paintings. The Palace area is divided into two parts: the Outer Court and the Inner Palace. The former consists of the first three main halls, where the emperor received his courtiers and conducted grand ceremonies, while the latter was the living quarters for the imperial residence. At the rear of the Inner Palace is the Imperial Garden where the emperor and his family sought recreation.

The main buildings, the six great halls, one following another, are set facing south along the central south-to-north axis from the Meridian Gate. On either side of the palace are many comparatively small buildings. Symmetrically in the northeastern section lie the six Eastern Palaces and in the northwestern section the six Western Palaces.

The Meridian Gate is the main entrance to the Palace. The emperor considered himself the "Son of the Heaven" and the Palace is the center of the universe, the south-to-north axis is just as the Meridian line going right through the Palace. The gate is crowned with five towers, known as the Five-Phoenix Towers, which were installed with drums and bells. When the emperor went to the Temple of Heaven, bells were struck to mark this important occasion. When he went to the Ancestral Temple, the drums were beaten in order to publicize the event.

Entering in the Meridian Gate you can see a vast courtyard, across which there is the Inner Golden Water River running from east to west. The river is spanned by five bridges, which were supposed to be symbols of the five virtues preached by Confucius—benevolence, righteousness, rites, intelligence, and fidelity

The Outer Court consists mainly of the Hall of Supreme Harmony, the Hall of Complete Harmony, and the Hall of Preserving Harmony, which are on a three-tiered white marble terrace, seven meters above the ground at the north end of the courtyard.

Among them, the most important hall in the palace complex was called the Hall of Supreme Harmony, which is rectangular in shape, 27 meters in height, 2,300 square meters in area, where the emperor held grand ceremonies, such as the Winter Solstice, the Spring Festival, the emperor's birthday and enthronement, and the dispatch of generals to battles, etc. On such occasions there would be an imperial guard of honor standing in front of the Hall that extended all the way to the Meridian Gate. It is also the largest existing palace of wooden structure in China.

The Forbidden City is an outstanding example of brilliant color combinations, such as yellow tiles, red or purple walls and colorful decorations. In ancient China different colors have different meanings. People can't use them freely. "Purple" refers to the Purple Palace in heaven, where the Heavenly Emperor resides; the emperor on earth is the Son of Heaven and should live in a palace compatible to the Purple Palace. Another meaning is that the word "purple" is actually a reference to the Thuban galaxy and also, an auspicious cloud, symbolizes the emperor. The princes' studies were allowed to use only green tiles because it was a residence for princes. Others didn't use yellow or red, they are only for emperors. The Chamber of Literary Profundity, for example, used black tiles because it was a library which is easily caught fire, and black, according to superstition, symbolized water, which can suppress fire.

On the eave rafter of the Hall of Supreme Harmony there are 10 beasts named dragon, phoenix, lion, Heavenly Steed, Sea Horse, Suanni, Yayu, Xiezhi, Douniu and Hangshi. All these animals are given certain meanings. Dragon and phoenix symbolize the emperor and empress; the Heavenly Steed and Sea Horse stand for the imperial power; Douniu and Yayu are believe to be able to create clouds and rains to extinguish a fire. Lion is the king of beast. Suanni is an imaginary beast preying on tigers and leopards, therefore symbolizes leadership. Xiezhi is believed to have sharp eyes to distinguish between right and wrong and therefore stand for the open and aboveboard character of the emperor. The last animal looks like a monkey named Hangshi who is used for preventing from thunder, which ranks 10th of the 10 mascots.

The Hall of Complete Harmony is smaller and square with windows on all sides. Here the emperor rehearsed for ceremonies. It is followed by the Hall of Preserving Harmony, in which banquets and imperial examinations were held.

The Inner Court is composed of the Palace of Heavenly Purity, the Hall of Union, and the Palace of Earthly Tranquility with three palaces on either side. Here the emperor used to handle daily state affairs and the empress and concubines used to live.

The Hall of Imperial Peace is in the center of the garden, which is a Taoist temple, with a flat roof slightly sloping down to the four eaves. This type of roof was rare in ancient Chinese architecture. In the garden there are hundreds of pines, cypresses and various flowers, so the garden all year round fills the air with flowers' fragrance. In the northeastern corner of the garden is a rock hill, known as the Hill of the Piled-up Wonders, on the top of which is a pavilion. At the foot of the hill are two fountains which jet two columns of water high into the air. It is said that on the ninth night of the ninth month of the lunar calendar, if a person climbs up a high place on that day, he would be safe from contagious diseases.

Folk legend has it that the Forbidden City has 9,999 and half rooms and the Imperial Palace in the heaven has 10,000 rooms. Emperor felt he would be inferior to the Heaven, therefore his palace had half a room less than in the heavenly palace.

Now the Forbidden City is no longer a forbidden place, it has become a public place for entertainment. Visiting the Palace Museum, you can enrich your knowledge of history, economy, politics, arts as well as architecture in ancient China and you can't tear yourself away.

OCABULARY ASSISTANT

the Meridian Gate 午门
the Five-Phoenix Towers 五凤楼
the Hall of Supreme Harmony 太和殿
the Hall of Complete Harmony 中和殿
the Hall of Preserving Harmony 保和殿
the Palace of Heavenly Purity 乾清宫
the Hall of Union 交泰殿
the Palace of Earthly Tranquility 坤宁宫
benevolence, righteousness, rites, intelligence, and fidelity 仁、义、礼、智、信
dragon, phoenix, lion, Heavenly Steed, Sea Horse, Suanni, Yayu, Xiezhi, Douniu and Hangshi 龙、凤、狮子、天马、海马、狻猊、押鱼、獬豸、斗牛、行什

1. When and why was the Palace Museum built?

2. How many emperors have lived in the Palace?

3. Describe the layout of the architecture.

4. Why did the emperor consider himself the "Son of the Heaven"?

5. What were the five bridges supposed to be symbolized?

6. Tell the function of the Hall of Supreme Harmony.

7. Tell the names of the Outer Palace and the Inner Palace.

8. Describe the Imperial Garden.

9. Why do natives of Beijing also call the Palace Museum the Forbidden City?

10. What do the beasts on the eave rafter of the Hall of Supreme Harmony represent?

5 Try to fill in the following chart about how to introduce the Palace Museum to the guests.

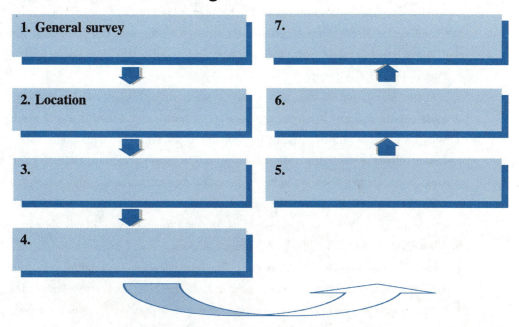

6 Rewrite the following passage into a dialogue and practice with your partners.

The Mascots of the Beijing 2008 Olympic Games

The Beijing Olympic Games was held on August 8th, 2008. In that time China became the spotlight of the whole world. As young ambassadors for the Olympic Games Fuwa-Friendlies were served as the Mascots of Beijing 2008 Olympic Games, carrying a message of friendship and peace to all over the world. They embody the natural characteristics of four of China's most popular animals—the Fish, the Panda, the Tibetan Antelope, the Swallow and the Olympic Flame. Each of Fuwa has a rhyming two-syllable name—a traditional way of expressing affection for children in China. Beibei is the Fish, Jingjing is the Panda, Huanhuan is the Olympic Flame, Yingying is the Tibetan Antelope and Nini is the Swallow. When you put their names together—Bei Jing Huan Ying Ni—that means "Welcome to Beijing", which offers a warm invitation that reflects the mission of Fuwa. Fuwa also embody both the landscape, the dreams and aspirations of Chinese people. In their origins and their headpieces, you can see the five elements of nature—the sea, forest, fire, the earth and the sky—all reflect the deep traditional influences of Chinese folk art and ornamentation. In the ancient culture of China, there is a grand tradition of spreading blessings through signs and symbols. Each of Fuwa symbolizes a different blessing: prosperity, happiness, passion, health and good luck. Fuwa will seek to unite the world in peace and friendship through the Olympic spirit. Its theme is "One World, One Dream," reflecting the deep desire of the Chinese people to reach out to the world in friendship through the Games—and to invite every man, woman and child to take part in the great celebration of human solidarity.

Beibei stands for the fish and water, symbolsizing prosperity and harvest in traditional culture and art. It carries the blessing of prosperity. A fish is also a symbol of surplus in Chinese culture, indicating another a good harvest and a good life. The ornamental lines of the water wave designs are taken from well-known Chinese paintings. Among Fuwa, Beibei is known to be gentle and pure, reflecting the blue Olympic ring.

Jingjing makes children smile—and that's why he brings the blessing of happiness wherever he goes. You can see his joy in the charming naivety of his dancing pose and the lovely wave of his black and white fur. As a national treasure and a protected species, pandas are adored by people. The lotus designs in Jingjing's headdress, which are inspired by the porcelain paintings of the Song Dynasty, symbolizing the lush forest and the harmonious relationship between man and nature. Jingjing was chosen to represent our desire to protect nature and environment. Because of Jingjing's charming appearance, optimistic spirit and full of vitality, he is an athlete noted for strength, representing the black Olympic ring.

Huanhuan is the big brother, symbolizing the Olympic Flame and the passion of sport. Huanhuan stands in the center of five Fuwa, representing the core embodiment of the Olympic spirit. Because he inspires all with the passion to run faster, jump higher and be stronger, he is also open and inviting. Wherever the light of Huanhuan shines, the inviting warmth of Beijing 2008 and the wishful blessings of the Chinese people can be felt. The lovely designs of his head ornament are drawn from the famed Dunhuang murals—with just a touch of China's traditional lucky designs. Huanhuan is outgoing and enthusiastic. He excels at all the ball games and represents the red Olympic ring.

Yingying is a fast and agile antelope, swiftly racing across the earth. A symbol of the vastness of China's landscape, the antelope carries the blessing of health, the strength of body that comes from harmony with nature. Yingying's flying pose captures the essence of a species unique to the Qinghai-Tibet Plateau, one of the first animals put under protection in China. Tibetan Antelope reflects Beijing commitment to a Green Olympics. His head ornament incorporates several decorative styles from the Qinghai-Tibet and Sinkiang cultures and the ethnic designs. In track and field events, Yingying is a quick-witted and agile boy, representing the yellow Olympic ring.

Nini's figure is drawn from this grand tradition of flying designs. Among the kite designs, the golden-winged swallow is traditionally one of the most popular. Her golden wings symbolize the infinite sky and spread good-luck as a blessing wherever she flies. Swallow is also pronounced "yan" in Chinese, and Yanjing is what Beijing was called as an ancient capital city. Among Fuwa, Nini is as innocent and joyful as a swallow. She is strong in gymnastics and represents the green Olympic ring.

7 Cultural Salon: Read the following passage, try to get some cultural knowledge about *Peking Opera* and answer the questions.

Peking Opera was originally a form of local theatre, which spread all over the country and then became the national opera of China. It is said that about 200 years ago, the Qing Emperor Qianlong toured in southern China and developed an interest in the local operas. On his 80th birthday, he let local opera troupes come to Beijing to perform for him. In 1781, artists from Anhui Province came into Beijing. By the mid-19th century, a local opera from Hubei Province was also introduced into Beijing. The two operas were often staged at the same time. Eventually, the ones from Anhui and Hubei were incorporated with the palace opera—Kunqu Opera, which formed a brand new opera—the Peking Opera. Peking Opera combines literature with singing, dancing, musical dialogues, martial arts, colorful facial make-up and fantastic costumes.

The music of Peking Opera is mainly orchestral music. The percussion instruments, in particular, provide a strongly rhythmical accompaniment to acting and make it extremely live and real.

Roles in Peking Opera

In Peking Opera the roles are divided into four main types according to the sex, age, social status, and profession of the character. They are Sheng, Dan, Jing and Chou.

Sheng refers to male roles, who are the leading male actors divided into scholars, officials, warriors, patriots, etc. It is subdivided into Lao sheng, who wear beards and represent old-aged men, Xiao sheng, a young men, Wu sheng with martial skills, Wen sheng are the scholar and public servants. Wawa Sheng refer to children.

Dan is regarded as female roles. They are subdivided into the Lao dan—the elderly, dignified ladies. The Qing yi—noble ladies in elegant costumes; the Hua dan—ladies' maids, usually in bright colored costumes who do more acting than singing; the Wu dan are horsewomen and warriors; the Lao dan refers to old ladies and the Cai dan, the female comedians, and sometimes shrews or dangerous women. The dan is usually considered the most important role on the stage.

Jing are the painted-faces roles. They represent warriors, heroes, statesmen, adventures and demons. The different colors and designs on the faces refer to different characteristics. According to the different social positions and characters, it is divided into several groups.

The Chou, or clown, can be recognized by the patch of white paint around his nose, sometimes outlined in black. so it also has a nickname—Xiao Hua Lian. The Chou roles represent foolish, awkward or stingy people, whose slangy remarks set everybody laughing.

1. When did Peking Opera appear?

2. What styles does Peking Opera have?

3. How many roles does Peking Opera have and what do they symbolize?

4. Do you like Peking Opera? Why or why not?

_____

5. How to develop Chinese Traditional arts?

_____

▎ *Further reading: Beijing Hutong*

Good morning, ladies and gentlemen, today I will show you around local custom in Beijing. I am sure you will like it. An understanding Beijing would surely be inadequate without knowing hutong. A hutong is an alley or lane typical in Beijing. Surrounding the Forbidden City, many hutongs were built during the Yuan (1206—1341), Ming (1368—1628) and Qing (1644—1908) dynasties. In the prime of these dynasties the emperors, in order to establish supreme power for themselves, planned the city and arranged the residential areas according to the etiquette systems of the Zhou Dynasty. The center of Beijing was the royal palace—the Forbidden City.

There are several opinions on the origin of the name hutong. One view holds that when Beijing was first built, in order to prevent spread of fire, residences are separated by a space called Fire Path, which was pronounced huolihuotong in Mongolian. Later, it was shorted to huotong and, finally, to hutong. A second opinion argues that in ancient times, Mongolians were called as hu. When the Mongolians set their capital in Beijing, they named the alley between residences hutong, which means harmony between Mongolians and Hans in order to promote unity. A more common view contends that the term derived from the Mongolian word of haote, meaning settlements of residents.

Statistics shows that there are 7,000 hutongs, with the widest being 4 meters and narrowest 70 cm, just enough space for a person to pass through. According to the 1990 edition of the Encyclopedia of Beijing, in the Eastern, Western, Chongwen and Xuanwu districts alone, there are 1,216 hutongs, but now some of them are pulled down and new buildings are set up. One kind of hutongs was near the palace to the east and west and arranged in orderly fashion along the streets. Most of the residents of these hutongs were imperial relatives and aristocrats. Another kind, the simple and crude hutong, was mostly located far to the north and south of the palace. The residents were merchants and other ordinary people.

The courtyard dwellings are essential for an understanding of the culture of Beijing. They are the traditional form of residence in Beijing. The main buildings in the hutong were almost quadrangular courtyard—a building complex formed by four houses around a quadrangular courtyard. The quadrangles varied in size and design according to the social status of the residents. The big quadrangles of high-ranking officials and wealthy merchants were specially built with roof beams and pillars all beautifully carved and painted, each with a front yard and back yard. However, the ordinary people's quadrangles were simply built with small gates and low houses. Hutongs, in fact, are passageways formed by many closely arranged quadrangles of different sizes. The specially built quadrangles all face the south for better lighting; as a result, a lot of hutongs run from east to west. Between the big hutongs many small ones went north and south for convenient passage. A house facing south is the most respectable. Since there is only one door leading into the courtyard, the courtyard is a world of its own. Rooms on the four sides within the compound all open their doors toward the yard. Generally speaking, the houses sitting on the north and facing the south were for master, because they are warm in winter and cool in summer. The houses on east, west and south are for the inferior persons, such as children, relatives and servants. The spacious courtyard is good for planting trees and flowers, as well as for raising birds and gold fish. Some wealthy families also build rockeries and cultivate bonsai to enjoy nature at home.

In recent years, the houses in many hutongs have been pulled down and replaced by modern buildings. Many dwellers have moved into new buildings. The hutong today is becoming into the scenic spot for tourists.

However, in the urban district of Beijing houses along hutongs still occupy one third of the total area, providing housing for half the population, so many hutongs have survived. In this respect, you still can enjoy both the ancient and the modern Beijing.

8 Work in Pairs.

Student A You are a European visitor to China.

Student B You are a tour guide.
Student A asks Student B to introduce the roles in Peking Opera.

9 Supplementary task: Introduce one of cities or ancient capitals you are interested in or talk about your hometown. Make a presentation in class. The teacher and students will comment on your presentation.

Unit 6 Chinese Ancient Gardens

AIMS

- To understand what and how to prepare for talking about a Chinese ancient garden
- To find ways to improve your guiding skills and performance
- To master the basic words and expressions of talking about a Chinese ancient garden
- To know the Chinese ancient garden's scenery, configuration and characteristics

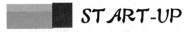

START-UP

Make a list of all the common words you know in introducing a Chinese ancient garden.

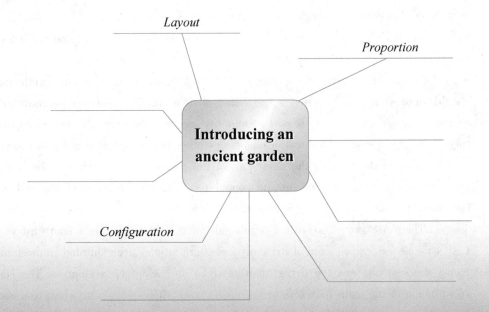

1 **Read the following passage and answer the questions.**

The Mountain Resort

Chengde Mountain Resort, also known as Rehe Imperial Palace for short stays away from the capital, was begun to build in the 42nd year of Emperor Kangxi(1703) in the Qing Dynasty. It ranks as the largest imperial garden in China, represents the essence of ancient gardening art, and leaves us a treasure of studying Chinese traditional culture. As a royal garden it embodies the prevalent garden styles in both north and south China and earns the fame of "gathering all the beautiful sceneries under the sun in one garden." From the geographic feature to the scenic spots distribution the garden is quite the same with the landform of China, so it can be looked as a miniature of our country.

In order to safeguard the unity of the multinational dynasticism and strengthen the northern frontier, in the 20th year of the reign of Kangxi, the Mulan Imperial Hunting Ground was built for the purpose of more political and military reasons than the onefold intention of hunting. It's about 150 km north of Chengde city and 384km away from the Forbidden City in Beijing. It's necessary to set up some palaces along the way from Beijing to the Hunting Ground as the temporary resting places; one of them is today's Mountain Resort.

The Mountain Resort is divided into two parts by natural condition: the palace area and the scenery area. Let's look around the palace area first. Now we are in the Hall of Frugality and Placidity—the place where emperors conducted state affairs; what inscribed on the board hung in the hall are four Chinese characters "Danbo Jingcheng" by Emperor Kangxi. Since the hall was built with Nanmu, it was also called Nanmu Hall. This rare species of wood can smell fancy aroma, people will feel vivifying on entering into the hall. Then we'll have a look at the Four Knowledge Study, the four characters were written by Qianlong. Sizhi means a trusting gentleman should know what is soft, hard, sublime and obvious. In this room, emperors interviewed the close officials and important minority leaders; the room also served as sitting-room for emperors taking rest or changing clothes before and after going to court.

Walking to the back is the inner part of the palace area, which was the living court for emperors and his queen and concubines. The middle room which used for the emperors' family life is the famous hall called the Hall of Coziness through Misty Waves. There are two courtyards to each side of this hall: the west courtyard was Cixi's living residence, some of her daily necessary articles are exhibited in the front room; the east one was the living quarters of Ci'an—Xianfeng's empress. The last construction of the main palace is Tower for Viewing Misty Mountain, where you can enjoy the view of beautiful misty mountains.

The scenery area is divided into three parts: the lake area, the plain area and the mountain area.

The lake area lies to the north of the palace buildings, occupies about 14% of the whole resort proportion, six times the size of the palace area, among the 72 scenic spots named by Kangxi and Qianlong, 31 ones are distributed in this area, which forms the main scenic outlook in the resort.

The three pavilions over the lake are called "Water Center Pavilions", modeled after the Huxinting pavilions in the West Lake of Hangzhou, Zhejiang Province. There is a causeway called Zigzag Path and Cloudy Dike, which connected with three islets: the Green Water Round islet on the left, the Lucky Jade Islet in the middle and the Hall of Enjoying Gurgling Stream in Moonlight Islet on the right. Ruyi Islet is the biggest of the three, to the north of the islet stands a 2-storeyed building named the Tower of Mist and Rain, which served as study of the emperors. At the east bank of the lake is the Lion Grove. It's just like a miniascape in the resort, so habitually called it "Garden in the Garden". Its designment is imitated the Lion Grove in Suzhou, the overall arrangement is unique with lion-like rockeries laying out the garden, and all the scenic spots are joined by stone steps and small bridges.

Now we come to the center of the Mountain Resort and also the highest building in the lake area—the Golden Hill, which modeled after the Jinshan Temple in Zhejiang, Jiangsu Province. The groundwork of the Hill was structured by a forest of rockeries. The three-storeyed hexagonal tower is the Tower of God, the emperors used to sacrifice the heaven here.

Rehe Spring is the main source of the lake water; the name was earned from its no freezing in winter. The water runs 300 meters to join the Wulie River; this distance is called Hot River. As the shortest river in the world, it is recorded in the Encyclopedia of Great Britain. What located on the west bank was a royal warehouse called Fragrant Garden. It is a courtyard where silver articles, silk works, and such like jewelries were housed. There was a market opened in the yard for the empress and concubines to look for fun and taste the pleasure of common people's life.

Wenjin Book Repository was built in 1774; it was listed as one of the four imperial libraries of the Qing Dynasty. The repository stored one set of the Complete Collection of the Four Treasures. The pond in front of Wenjin Book Repository is called Banyuechi-accompanying-moon pond, in the sunny day you can see a crescent moon reflected in the water. This wonder comes from the mighty works of the rockeries nearby; the sunshine passing through a crescent-shaped hole in a rockery makes the artificial moon mirrored in the water.

Plain Area

We are now in the plain area.

The plain area lies to the north of the lakes. For remaining its natural state, few man-made buildings can be found here. The grand grassland extending before us is called Ten-Thousand-Tree Garden, the Mongolian yurts were set up on this land, and it is here that Emperor Qianlong received Mongolian princes, Tibetan Panchen Lama and British envoy, McCartney.

There is a Buddhist temple on the grassland named the Temple for Ever Blessing. Sitting in the temple yard is the Six Harmonies Pagoda, Liuhe in Buddhism means the harmonies of the heaven, earth, east, west, south and north. On each storey of this nine-layer and 67 meter-high stupa a Buddha is enshrined.

Mountain District

The mountain area is in the west over there.

The mountain area covers 4/5 area of the entire resort. There once were more than 40 sights in Kangxi and Qianlong reign, but most of them had been destroyed. Lying from south to north are four valleys. The Fancinating View Tower is one of the sights in the first valley; on the top one can have an enchanting view of the mountains and waters. The Pavilion of Sunset over the Sledge Hammer Peak is another gallant site, standing here you can enjoy the fancy view—the great rock club in distance at the sunsetting time. In the second valley, there was a Zhuyuansi Temple which was demolished by Japanese invaders in 1943, now only the temple gate and the bell tower survived. The Pavilion surrounded by Cloud-Enclosed Mountains and the Pavilion of Viewing the Snow-Capped South Mountains are the two main outlooks of the third and fourth valley.

The Mountain Resort contains all the points that the royal gardens should involve: broad in scope, magnificent in construction, strong imperial symbolization. All the gardening arts in both south and north, royal and folk are well displayed in this garden.

VOCABULARY ASSISTANT

distribution 分布
aroma 芳香
causeway 铺道
crescent 月牙
Panchen Lama 班禅喇嘛
Wenjin Book Repository 文津阁
Temple for Ever Blessing 永佑寺

dynasticism 王朝统治
sublime 庄严
miniascape 盆景
encyclopedia 百科全书
Green Water Round 环碧
Six Harmonies Pagoda 六和塔
Fancinating View Tower 绮望楼

CHINESE ANCIENT GARDENS UNIT 6   63

> Four Knowledge Study 四知书屋   Tower of Mist and Rain 烟雨楼
> Water Center Pavilions 水心榭   Zigzag Path and Cloudy Dike 云径芝堤
> Enjoying Gurgling Stream in Moonlight 月色江声
> the Hall of Frugality and Placidity 澹泊敬诚殿
> the Hall of Coziness through Misty Waves 烟波致爽殿
> The Pavilion of Sunset over the Sledge Hammer Peak 锤峰落照
> Snow-Capped South Mountains 南山积雪

1. What is the characteristic of China's imperial garden?
_____

2. Why is the Mountain Resort looked as a miniature of our country?
_____

3. Could you name some important historical events happened in the Mountain Resort?
_____

4. For what reasons and the real purposes were the Mountain Resort built?
_____

5. What does Liuhe (six harmonies) stand for?
_____

2 Fill in the gaps with a suitable word from the box. Change their forms if necessary.

| model after | crescent moon | fancy aroma | imperial | study |
| sacrifice | miniature | valley | royal garden | freezing |

1. Chengde Mountain Resort lists as the largest _____ garden in China.
2. It can be looked as a _____ of our country.
3. Nanmu Hall can smell _____.
4. The Tower of Mist and Rain served as _____ of the emperors.
5. "Water Center Pavilions" _____ the Huxinting pavilions in the West Lake of Hangzhou.
6. The Tower of God is a place for the emperors to _____ the heaven.
7. In the sunny day you can see a _____ reflected in accompanying-moon pond.
8. There are four _____ in the mountain area.
9. The Mountain Resort contains all the points that the _____ should involve.
10. The name Rehe was earned from its no _____ in winter.

3 Talk about the famous scenic spots in Chengde Mountain Resort.

Golden Hill

Rehe Spring

Hall of Frugality and Placidity

Six Harmonies Pagoda

4 Read the following passage and answer the questions.

The Humble Administrator's Garden

The Humble Administrator's Garden is the largest ancient garden in Suzhou, which was built in 1509, the 4th year of Emperor Zhengde, Ming Dynasty. It ranks with the Lingering Garden in Suzhou, the Summer Palace in Beijing and the Mountain Resort in Chengde as the most famous Chinese ancient gardens. The former two in Suzhou keep as the typical private gardens, while the latter two are ones served for imperial or official use. The Humble Administrator's Garden is a masterpiece of the Chinese gardening in Ming Dynasty and enjoys great reputation in all the ancient gardens in China. Three-fifth of its area is taken up by water, which forms the key feature of this garden. The distinctive styles of the garden are reflected in its layout, mold-making, elegant sculptures and many other aspects. More than this, the garden used to be the function place attended by some very important persons in history, Li Xiucheng in Taiping Tianguo, Li Hongzhang in the Qing Dynasy, after Anti-Japanese War, the poet Liu Yazi set up a college here, all these help to boost the garden's distinction. It was listed as the world culture heritage by UNESCO in 1997.

The Humble Administrator's Garden was set up by a high-rank official named Wang Xianchen. When lost court favor, he retired to Suzhou and turned to nature for sympathy. In Wang's understanding the life of planting trees, watering flowers, growing vegetables, meeting friends and doing suchlike things was a career of a humble administrator, so came the garden's name.

The garden consists of three parts, east, west and central. The east part named Back to the Fields Garden was ignored long before, the facilities such as teahouses, gates were re-equipped in 1955 by government, the whole garden is an integrated landscape. Now the pools, pavilions, islets, bamboo houses and green land decorate the eastern district a brilliant view, and turn this land a real taste of rural scenery.

The west sights center on a pool, the Hall of 36 Mandarin Ducks lies to the north part, looking from outside it is one big hall, in fact there are two living rooms inside, the north one was served to enjoy the cool in summer and the south to warm in winter, the host used to rest, meet friends and listen to the operas in this hall. The Hall of 18 Camellias lies to the south, offered as female rooms, so high walls were built around to block the outside world into the girls' view. Another finely designed scenic spot in this area is the Pavilion of Remain-and-Listen; it is a one-floor hall with windows on the four sides. What're worth seeing in this pavilion are the tridimensional sculptural articles from gingko wood, the lifelike pine, bamboo and plum flowers, they are the works of the Qing Dynasty. Almost at the end of the west part of the garden a unique sight catches our eye—the Pagoda Shadow Pavilion, though it does not stand on the noticeable position, yet leaves us no less impression. The pavilion, the trees, the rockeries and the shadows mirrored in the water make this corner outstanding.

The center part draws visitors' attention more, the most attracting building is the Hall of Distant Fragrance, and it is the main body in this area. There are no pillars inside the hall, the latticed glass windows are symmetrically fixed in all the four sides. Sitting in the hall one can indulge viewing the landscapes in all directions, Xiuqi Pavilion in the east, Yiyu Veranda in the west, a rockery in the south and a lotus pond in the north. Numbers of potted plants laid out inside with the environment outside make the hall picturesque and charming, though artificial yet natural. In summer the fragrance of the flowers pervades the hall and spreads further away, so earning such a name. There keeps the longest couplets in Suzhou gardens, 80 characters in total, on which recorded the grand occasions of high officials' gathering. A stone bridge named Little Flying Rainbow lies to the west of Yuanxiangtang, the inverted vermeil railing reflected in the water makes a rainbow-like scene, and the name comes from this wonderful view. It is the only covered bridge in Suzhou gardens. The Fragrant Islet is a skillfully designed ship-like building, a plaque with two Chinese characters Xiangzhou carved on the top of it, which is out of the hands of the great calligrapher Wen Zhengming, Ming Dynasty. This islet is the main sight and also the symbol of the garden.

The Humble Administrator's Garden represents the garden's building style of the Ming Dynasty, not too simple yet elegant, full of quiet vitality. It embodies the comprehensive elements of the private gardens. The builder tried to make artificially a small world of their own, so all the points of an ideal living surroundings should be involved in one construction. They intended to create a landscape that could include as many beautiful types of scenery as possible in the limited space, the well-arranged rockeries, bridges, ponds and pavilions will give people the feeling that they live in a harmonious manmade nature.

OCABULARY ASSISTANT

sculpture 雕刻
mandarin duck 鸳鸯
gingko 银杏
Lingering Garden 留园
Hall of 18 Camellias 十八曼陀罗花馆
Pagoda Shadow Pavilion 塔影亭
Hall of Distant Fragrance 远香堂
Little Flying Rainbow 小飞虹

imperial 皇帝的
tridimensional 立体的
calligrapher 书法家
Back to the Fields Garden 归田园
Remain-and-Listen 留听阁
Xiuqi Pavilion 绣绮亭
Yiyu veranda 倚玉轩
Fragrant Islet 香洲

1. Who built the Humble Administration Garden and why did he build it?

2. What is the key feature of this garden?

3. Could you say something about the architectural style of the Ming Dynasty?

4. Which part is your favorite in this garden? Why?

5. How many parts does the Humble Administrator's Garden consist of? What are they?

6. How to tell the guests the characteristics of the private gardens?

7. How does the name Little Flying Rainbow come from?

8. Which part of the garden is more attracting visitor's attention?

_____

9. What's the building feature of the Hall of Distant Fragrance?

_____

10. Could you name some other private gardens?

_____

5 **Try to fill in the following chart about how to introduce the Humble Administrator's Garden to the guests.**

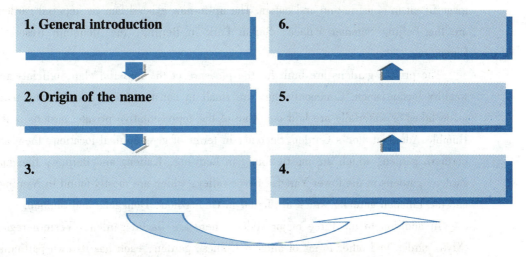

1. General introduction	6.
2. Origin of the name	5.
3.	4.

6 **Rewrite the following passage into a dialogue and practice with your partners.**

> The usage of a garden is to meet man's demand for relaxation and lodging. A Chinese garden mixes man-made landscape with natural scenery, painting, architecture and such like arts together. The classical gardens are made by recreating the splendors of natural scenery through the processes of land decoration, such as planting trees, shrubs and flowers, designing and materializing mountains and watercourses. To some extend, it is a landscape painting in three dimensions. So a Chinese garden is not just a park or something attached to a building. It is the world in miniature. By reconstructing nature, the Chinese gardens reflect the nature scenes.
>
> The creation of classical gardens depends on mountains, rivers, buildings, plants and animals. In these gardens the ground is usually like that of a mountain area. This kind of garden layout imitates real terrain. Halls, verandas, pavilions and bridges blend well with the real mountains and rivers. The surroundings of the classical gardens provide a natural sense for visitors and let people enjoy the beauty and stillness of nature.

Now there are about 1000 classical gardens in China. The most important examples are located in Beijing, Chengde and Suzhou. They stand out uniquely among the world gardens and make some valuable contribution to the cultural heritage of mankind.

The system of Chinese classical gardens is so profound that the experts have failed to reach an agreement of how to type its categories. Generally, there are two major ways to classify Chinese gardens. First, according to the ownerships of the gardens, they can be classified into imperial gardens and private gardens. The former are characterized by large-scale, more real mountains and rivers, tall body building, and magnificent in construction and colors. The up-to-now existed famous imperial gardens are the Beijing Summer Palace, Beihai Park in Beijing, the Mountain Resort in Chengde.

The private gardens are built for the pleasure of the imperial clan, officials and wealthy businessmen. Commonly they are small in construction, rockeries and man-made lakes or waterfalls are laid out. One of the representative private gardens is the Humble Administrator's Garden. Second, in terms of geographical location, there are northern garden, which are mostly found in Luoyang, Kaifeng and Beijing; Jiangnan garden, gardens in the lower Yangtze River valley, which are mostly found in Nanjing; and the Lingnan garden, which are found in Guangzhou, Dongguan and Shunde.

In addition to the three major styles, there are Bashu garden, Western region (Xiyu) garden and other forms of ancient Chinese garden, each has its own particular features.

7 **Cultural Salon: Read the following passage, try to get some cultural knowledge about *Chinese tea* and answer the questions.**

Tea is the most extensive drinks in the world; it is simple but not insipid, so nearly every country, especially the East, has the habit of drinking tea. This is a tradition of life as well as of culture. Historical documents record that tea was first produced in China, however the exact age couldn't be run down for its too long history,

and one accepted data is traced back to the period of the Warring States. China has the greatest variety types of tea in the world, yet up to now, no standard approach is made out to classify these different classes. Generally, tea can be divided into six major categories. They are green tea, black tea, scented tea, oolong tea, white tea and pressed tea.

Categories of Tea

Green tea is not fermented, it has the longest history and lists top one in output, the leaves and soup are green, so gets the name. People enjoy its fresh taste and natural fragrant smell. Famous green tea includes Longjing (Dragon Well) Tea from the West Lake in Hangzhou, Yunwu (Cloud and Mist) Tea from Lushan Mountain, Yinzhen (Silver Needle) Tea from Junshan Mountain, Maofeng Tea from Huangshan Mountain. Black tea is fully fermented with "red" leaves and "red" soup, in the process of fermentation, the tea turns from green to black. Scented tea, which smells of flowers, is made by mixing green tea with flower petals through elaborate working way, jasmine, rose and plum all can be used as black tea materials. Oolong tea is semi-fermented; the leaf of this kind of tea is green in center with red edge around. The main producing areas are Fujian, Guangdong and Taiwan. Oolong tea possesses both the nature of black tea and green tea, mellowness and freshness, it becomes more and more welcomed especially by Japanese. White tea gets the name from its white color and clear water, it is not fermented and the leaves are not kneaded. The main producing places are Fuding and Zhenhe, Fujian Province. The pressed tea is of special kind. Putting steamed green tea, black tea or scented tea into brick or ball shape tools and pressed then out of this type of tea, it's a favorite for people in the remote areas for its convenience in taking. It mainly produced in Yunnan, Sichuan, Hunan and Hubei.

Whichever type the tea is, the leaves all come from the evergreen bushes in the hilly areas in China, and proper climatic and soil conditions are needed when growing tea. The manner of drinking tea is an indispensable part in tea culture. Different countries or regions have the different tea-drinking way. In China, the Han nationality prefers to drink natural flavor plain tea, while some minorities enjoy drinking tea with milk mixed. China is the first country to find tea drinkable as well as its medical and healthy functions. It's good to drink tea moderately, but if overdrinking side effects may happen, such as stomach disorder or sleeplessness.

> Water and tea set are both important while drinking tea, to say savoring tea is much better. A quiet, neat and comfortable place is certainly desirable, so tea-house sprung up with drinking tea tradition. Snatching a bit of leisure from a busy schedule, making a kettle of strong tea can drive yourself out from fatigue and make you less strained.

1. How many categories does tea have according to the introduction?

2. Could you introduce the qualities of these different kinds of tea?

3. What are other functions of drinking tea besides satisfying our thirst?

4. Which kind of tea do you enjoy savoring? Give your reasons.?

5. Why is pressed tea more acceptable in remote regions?

■ Further reading: Chinese Silk

> Silk has always been valued and prized for its sheen, light, duration, transparence and luminosity. It is one of the best clothing materials that none others can be matched, so reputed as the "queen" of fabrics. China is the first country to breed silkworms and produce silk, cocoons and pieces of silk have been unearthed among relics from 4,700 BC. The man-plough and woman-weave time in ancient China improved the silk production skill and spread it to other countries quickly.
>
>
>
> Our ancestors not only invented silk but used it in the costumes, economics and art, for this reason the Greeks called China the Silk Country. The great Silk Road was the most important connection between the Orient and the West—starting from Chang'an (Xi'an today) and ending at the eastern shore of the Mediterranean Sea. It linked up fields, deserts, grasslands and mountains. From this road, some Chinese

invented things were carried to the West, while Buddhism, Islam and their related arts were brought back.

With the development of silk technology, different varieties of silk fabric appear, the best known include damask, satin, raw silk, tough silk, embroidered silk and painted silk. This old but not out of date production still has its large market and lively vitality nowadays; many famous paintings are reproduced precisely with needles and silk threads. Embroidery is done with colored silk thread in various designed stitches. There are several important embroidery centers in China, each has their own particular characters, Suzhou embroidery is famous for its extremely delicate stitches, Xiang for its rich colors and Yue for its complicated patterns. It usually takes an artist several months or even years to complete a high quality great piece, so the value is also obvious.

China's three best known brocades are: Song brocade (宋锦) made in Suzhou, Shu brocade (蜀锦) made in Sichuan and Yun brocade (云锦) from Nanjing. They are the outstanding representatives of China's silk and still enjoy a high reputation in the world today. In a sense, silk adds to prove the long and splendid history of China.

8 Work in Pairs.

Student A You are a European visitor to China.

Student B You are a tour guide.

Student A asks Student B to introduce the categories of tea.

9 Supplementary task: Introduce one of Chinese ancient gardens you are interested in. Make a presentation within ten minutes in class. The teacher and students will make comments on if you address the main points and how the presentation can be improved.

Unit 7

Humane Landscapes

AIMS

- To understand what and how to prepare for talking about Humane Landscapes (The Great Wall, Mausoleums and Grottoes)
- To find ways to improve your guiding skills and performance
- To master the basic words and expressions of the Great Wall, Mausoleums and Grottoes
- To know how to introduce the Great Wall, Mausoleums and Grottoes

START-UP

Make a list of all the common words you know about the Great Wall.

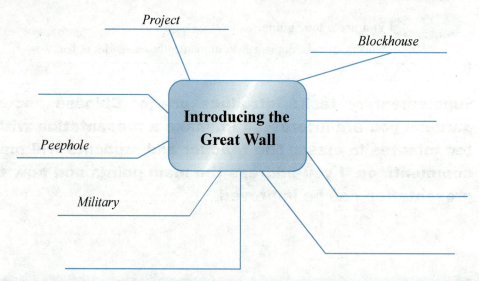

1 Read the following speech *The Great Wall* and answer the questions.

Ladies and Gentlemen, welcome to China.

Today we will visit the Great Wall. The Great Wall, one of the famous wonders of the world, is said to be the most conspicuous human work on earth that can be seen from outer space. The Great Wall of China was an ancient gigantic defensive project. It is one of the largest construction projects ever completed. Located in northern China, the Great Wall starts from Shanhaiguan Pass along the coast of the Bohai Sea in the east and ends in Jiayuguan Pass in Gansu Province in the west, traveling about 12,700 kilometers across Liaoning, Hebei, Beijing, Shanxi, Shaanxi, Inner Mongolia, Ningxia and Gansu. So we call the Great Wall "10,000-li wall". It winds its way westward over the vast territory of China from the bank of the Yalu River in Liaoning Province and ends at the foot of snowcapped Qilianshan and Tianshan mountains.

During the Warring States, the various rivaling states built city walls on their territory, considering self-defense. These walls were the precursors to the Great Wall. In 221 BC, Emperor Qinshihuang united China. To stop invading the Hans, he ordered to connect and extend the sections of walls built by Qin, Zhao and Yan in the north. After the Ming Dynasty superseded the Yuan Dynasty, the Mongolians continued to invade the Hans. At the same time, the Nuchen (Nǔzhēn) nationality was rising in the northeast. These posed serious threats to Ming rulers. It took the Ming Dynasty 200 years to complete all the construction and renovation of the Great Wall. What we see today is mostly the Ming Dynasty's Great Wall. In 1987 The Great Wall was listed by UNESCO as one of the World Cultural Heritages. The section at Jinshanling is the best part of the Great Wall, especially for its peculiar strategic passes.

The Jinshanling section of the Great Wall refers to the section beginning from the Wangjinglou Blockhouse in the east to the Longyu Pass in the west. Located at Luanping County in Hebei Province, 130 kilometers from Beijing, it is a major section of the ancient structure built over 2,000 years ago and also the hallmark of Great Wall in the Ming Dynasty.

Stretching on the two hills, the Grand Jinshanling and the Lesser Jinshanling, this part of the Great Wall is given the name of the Great Wall at Jinshanling. It was built in 1567 to guard the capital against the invaders from the north. It took 5 years to complete this great project.

Being a principal part of the Great Wall, it was carefully designed and strongly constructed along the mountains. With an average height of 7 meters, the wall is 6 meters wide at the base and 5 meters wide at the top. On the top of the wall bristle about 100 blockhouses. The blockhouses vary in shapes, such as square, oval, round and so on, even their roofs were varied, such as flat, domed, vaulted, quadrangular and octagonal. Most of them have vivid and beautiful names, such as Fairy Tower, General Tower, Watching Beijing Tower, the Big Fox-head Tower and so on. The blockhouses were built for various purposes. Some served as fighting places, some as storerooms and some as bed rooms. Among these blockhouses, "Kongxintai" is the best. It has two stories. The upper part serves as a shelter for soldiers on watch and the lower part, with six complicated passage-ways and doors opening to different directions, is rather like a maze, where enemies can be attacked easily.

The screen wall with the unicorn relievo on the top of the small Fox-head Tower is one of characteristics of the Great Wall. The unicorn is a kind of supernatural beast in the Chinese ancient fable and symbolized auspicious.

The barrier walls, called "Zhangqiang", another characteristic of construction rarely seen in other sections of the Great Wall, are a series of small walls on top of the Great Wall. They have peepholes and firing holes used to prevent the enemy from going ahead and approaching the blockhouses.

There is a 500-meter-long section of Great Wall laid by bricks with Chinese characters, which records the designation of the military units and ages. It is the third characteristic and the unique section of the Great Wall. It offers irrefutable facts to further study the Great Wall and has great values of cultural relics and scientific research.

At the east end of the Jinshanling Great Wall there is a famous blockhouse named Watching Beijing Tower, which was built on the peak of the Jinshanling Hill, nearly 1,000 meters above sea level. Perching on the highest peak, one could see the city walls of Beijing in the morning and the twinkling lights of Beijing in the evening. Looking around, one can catch sight of a vast view: to the east of the Great Wall, the Wuling Mountain; to the south, the Reservoir of Miyun; to the west, the Wohuling Hill; and to the north, wave upon wave of mountains. Though the Great Wall is no use for military defense today, it is still the best example of the Ming Great Wall and the great work of human beings.

As a culture treasure, the Great Wall is a symbol of Chinese civilization. It not only concentrated the blood and sweat of the ancient Chinese working people, but also embodied the intelligence, wisdom and creativeness of the ancient Chinese people. This is why it continues to be so attractive to the people both at home and abroad.

HUMANE LANDSCAPES UNIT 7

VOCABULARY ASSISTANT

conspicuous 显著的	blockhouse 碉堡	stretch 伸展
principal 主要的	bristle 竖起	peephole 窥视孔
run its course 按常规发展	perch 位于	military 军事的

1. Where does the Great Wall begin and where does it end?
_____

2. Which part is the most dangerous part of the Great Wall?
_____

3. What are the functions of the barrier walls?
_____

4. What are the characteristics of the Great Wall at Jinshanling?
_____

5. When was the Great Wall listed as one of the World Cultural Heritages by UNESCO?
_____

2 Fill in the gaps with a suitable word from the box. Change their forms if necessary.

defensive	territory	heritage	invader	approach
bristle	symbol	embody	complete	shelter

1. On the top of the wall _____ about 100 blockhouses and fighting platforms.
2. It winds its way westward over the vast _____ of China from the bank of the Yalu River and ends at the foot of snow-capped Qilianshan and Tianshan mountains.
3. The Great Wall of China was an ancient gigantic _____ project.
4. In 1987 The Great Wall was listed by UNESCO as one of the World Cultural _____.
5. The upper part serves as a _____ for soldiers on watch.
6. They have peepholes and firing holes used to prevent the enemy from going ahead and _____ the blockhouses.
7. It took 5 years to _____ this great project.
8. It was built in 1567 (the Ming Dynasty) to guard the capital against the _____ from the north.
9. As a culture treasure, the Great Wall is a _____ of Chinese civilization.
10. It _____ the intelligence, wisdom and creativeness of the ancient Chinese people.

3 Talk about the famous scenic spots of the Great Wall.

The Barrier Walls

Watching Beijing Tower

The Bricks with Chinese Characters

Blockhouses

4 Read the following passage and answer the questions.

The Mausoleum of Qin Shihuang

Known as Chang'an in ancient times, Xi'an is the capital city and the political, economic, cultural and transportation center of Shaanxi Province. It is also one of the newly industrialized bases in China. Historically, 11 dynasties set their capital here across a time span of 1,000 years, including Zhou, Qin, Han and Tang Dynasties. It is the only city in China as the capital with such a long history. In ancient times, Xi'an was the cultural center of Asia and the largest city in the world. The starting point of the famous Silk Road, Xi'an was matched only by Rome, which represented Western civilization. For this reason, Xi'an was listed as one of the four ancient capitals in the world at that time.

Why did so many dynasties choose Xi'an as their capital? This is because Xi'an is strategically located in the Guanzhong Plains, a fertile region of abundance. Also, in ancient times, the greatest threat to China came from the northwest, and Xi'an was the center of national defense. Geographically, the city occupies a crucial position in a corridor extending from east to west. Finally, having already served as a capital for many dynasties, Xi'an became a primary choice as capital for later dynasties.

There are many attractions in Xi'an, such as the Banpo Matriarchal Village, the Mausoleum of Qin Shihuang, the Huaqing Hot Springs and so on. Among them, the life-sized terra-cotta warriors and horses in the Mausoleum of Qin Shihuang have won the fame as one of the greatest archaeological find in 20th century.

In March 1974, peasants in Lintong County, 30 kilometers east of Xi'an, came across a piece of an earthen figure when digging a well, leading to the great discovery of terra-cotta warriors and horses which is a part of the Mausoleum of Qin Shihuang. In 1976, No.2 Vault and No.3 Vaults were found 20 meters away from No.1 Vault respectively after the drilling survey. In May 1976, Prime Minister Lee Kuan Yew of Singapore exclaimed, "This is a wonder in the world and a pride of the Chinese nation!" during a trip to the museum. In September 1978, Jacques Chirac, the former French president, commented after visiting the museum, "There were Seven Wonders of the World in the past, but I'd like to say this is the eighth Wonder of the World. A trip to China would be meaningless without visiting the terra-cotta warriors and horses."

Qin Shihuang, also called Ying Zheng, was the first emperor in the Qin Dynasty. He was enthroned at the age of 13, and took the helm of the state at the age of 22. By 221 B.C., he unified the six rival principalities of Qi, Chu, Yan, Han, Zhao and Wei, and established the first feudal empire in China's history. He named himself Shihuang Di, the first emperor in the Qin Dynasty. Since then, the supreme feudal rulers of China's dynasties had continued to call themselves Huang Di, the emperor.

Emperor Qin Shihuang's Mausoleum has not yet been excavated. What looks like inside could only be known when it is opened. However, the three vaults of the terra-cotta warriors and horses excavated can make one imagine how magnificent and luxurious the structure of Emperor Qin Shihuang's Mausoleum was. Standing 76 meters high against the slopes of Mt. Lishan and facing the Huishui River, the mausoleum was built in 247 B.C. when Qin Shihuang ascended the throne at the age of 13.

The magnificent underground palace is divided into two parts called the inner and outer cities. The inner city is a square and the outer is a rectangle, 2,500 meters wide and 6,200 meters long. It took over 700,000 people 36 years to build it. In 1979, 1989 and 1994, three vaults were officially open to the public.

No.1 Vault was stumbled upon in March 1974. In 1975, No.1 Vault, a museum covering an area of 16,300 square meters, was built with the permission of the State Council. The museum was formally opened to public on Oct. 1st, the National Day,

1979. The terra-cotta warriors and horses are arrayed according to the Qin Dynasty battle formation, symbolizing the troops keeping vigil beside the mausoleum. This discovery aroused much interest both at home and abroad.

No.2 Vault is about half the size of No.1 Vault, covering about 6,000 square meters. This is a composite formation of infantry, cavalry and chariot soldiers, from which roughly over 1,000 clay warriors, 500 chariots and saddled horses could be unearthed. The wooden chariots are already rotten, but their shafts, cross yokes and wheels, left clear impressions on the earth bed. The copper parts of the chariots still remain. Each chariot is pulled by four horses which are one and half meters high and two meters long.

No.3 Vault covers an area of 520 square meters with 69 warriors carrying defensive weapons and a wooden chariot pulled by four magnificent horses, supposed to be the command post of the battle formation.

All of the clay warriors in the three vaults held real weapons in their hands and face east, showing Emperor Qin Shihuang's strong determination of wiping out the six states and unifying the whole country.

From the terra-cotta army vaults, thousands of real weapons were unearthed, such as broad knives, swords, spears, dagger-axes, halberds, bows, crossbows and arrowheads. These weapons were exquisitely made. Some of them are still very sharp. Analyses show that they are made of alloys of copper and tin, containing more than ten kinds of other metals. Since their surfaces were treated with chromium, they are as bright as new, though buried underground for over 2,000 years. This indicates that the Qin Dynasty's metallurgical technology and weapon-manufacturing technique already reached a high level.

The figures vary from one another in expression, clothes, color, posture and hairstyle. Some are standing, some are kneeling. The way to distinguish between officers and soldiers is whether they wear hats. The officers all wear hats, but soldiers don't. Senior officers wear colored scaled armor; intermediate-level officers wear colored, yellow-brimmed front or side armor; and low-ranking officers wear plain armors. Soldiers' armor is larger in size and fewer in number of plates than that of officers. The terra-cotta warriors display a unique personality from their expressions. The generals stand tall and strong, scintillating with wisdom and sophistication; officers look serious, staunch and clam; the soldiers are alert, brave and dauntless.

The chariots and horses are decorated with colored drawings against white background. They have been fitted with more than 1,500 pieces of gold and silvers and decorations, looking luxurious, splendid and graceful. Probably they were meant for the use of Emperor Qin Shihuang's soul to go on inspection. The bronze chariots and horses were made by lost wax casting, which shows a high level of technology. For instance, the tortoise-shell-like canopy is about 4mm thick, and the window is only 1mm thick on which are many small holes for ventilation.

According to a preliminary study, the technology of manufacturing the bronze chariots and horses has involved casting, welding, reveting, inlaying embedding and chiseling. The excavation of the bronze chariots and horses provides extremely valuable material and data for the textual research of the metallurgical technique, the mechanism of the chariot and technological modeling of the Qin Dynasty.

The Mausoleum is an important archaeological discovery in the world, which is a valuable file for further study of the politics, military affairs, economy, culture and art of the Qin Dynasty. Chinese art critics consider the excavation of the 2,000-year-old terra-cotta figures an unprecedented event in the history of both Chinese and world sculpture.

OCABULARY ASSISTANT

civilization 文明　　　archaeological 考古学的　　　mausoleum 王的陵墓
excavate 挖掘　　　　array 部署　　　　　　　　　cavalry 骑兵
exquisitely 精巧地　　chromium 铬　　　　　　　　chariot 战车
chiseling 砍凿　　　　metallurgical 冶金学的

1. Who was Emperor Qin Shihuang?

2. Where is the Emperor Qin Shihuang's Mausoleum located?

3. Describe the layout of the architecture.

4. Why did Emperor Qin Shihuang build the Mausoleum?

5. How were the terra-cotta warriors and horses discovered?

6. What do the terra-cotta warriors and horses symbolize?

7. Respectively describe No.1 Vault, No.2 Vault and No.3 Vault.

8. What are the characteristics of the terra-cotta warriors?

UNIT 7 HUMANE LANDSCAPES

9. What kinds of the technology of manufacturing the bronze chariots and horses were used?

10. Why do people say the Mausoleum is an important archaeological discovery in the world?

5 **Try to fill in the following chart about how to introduce the Mausoleum of Emperor Qin Shihuang to the guests.**

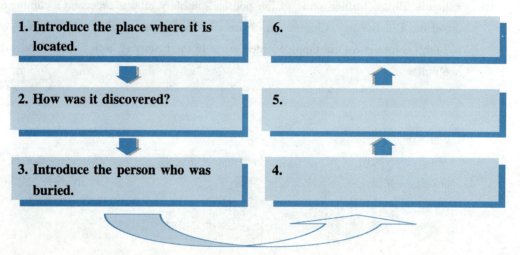

1. Introduce the place where it is located.
2. How was it discovered?
3. Introduce the person who was buried.
4.
5.
6.

6 **Rewrite the following passage into a dialogue and practice with your partners.**

Dunhuang Mogao Grottoes

Dunhuang Mogao Grottoes, commonly called One-Thousand-Buddha Caves, is about 1,600 meters along the eastern side of the Mingsha Mountain, 25 kilometers away from Dunhuang in Gansu Province. It was listed as one of the UNESCO world heritages in 1987. Dunhuang Mogao Grottoes are the biggest grotto art museum in China, followed by the Longmen Grottoes in Luoyang, Henan Province, and the Yungang Grottoes in Datong, Shanxi Province. They are the three biggest grottoes in China and the best preserved treasure houses of Buddhist art in the world.

Dunhuang Mogao Grottoes is hewn from a steep cliff at the foot of Mingsha Mountain. It is five stories in height and more than 1,600 meters in length from north to south. It was said that the Dunhuang area was a marshland 1,000 years ago. A monk named Yue Zun had a vision of 1,000 golden Buddhas when he was traveling through the area in 366 A.D., so he decided to turn his vision into a reality.

The carving project began in 366 A.D., the second year of the reign of Jianyuan of the pre-Qin Dynasty. Later Emperor Wu Zetian ruled China and expanded a lot of caves and niches, the number of caves and niches had reached more than 1,000. Forty years ago, these oldest Buddhist grottoes were in serious disrepair. The interior of all the grottoes had been severely damaged by wind and water erosion, and many grottoes had even collapsed by man and nature through the centuries. Smoke obscured the murals and time had eaten away the painted surfaces. Without the half-century's hard conservation work by a team of chemists, geologists and experts, most grottoes might well have been reduced to total ruin by this time. Today there are 492 grottoes left, including 45,000 square meters mural paintings, 2,415 colored sculptures and more than 4,000 flying apsarases painted on the ceilings. In addition there are five wooden buildings from the Tang and Song dynasties and 50,000 documents and cultural relics.

Murals from various periods reflecting social life, clothing, production, ancient architecture, music, dance and acrobatics, are a historical record of cultural exchanges between China and other regions. The murals of the Mogao Grottoes are of high historical and artistic value. Those from the Tang Dynasty achieve the highest artistic perfection with strong figures that are well shaped and proportioned and featuring attractive lively images. The images in the grottoes are a valuable reference for the study of ancient Chinese society from the fourth century to the 14th century.

The painted statues in the Dunhuang Grottoes focus on integration of color and form. Bright colors exaggerate the characteristics of the subjects. The statues and portraits of Buddhist worshippers wear the dresses and ornaments of different nationalities and classes, showing how ancient people were dressed and how they influenced each other mutually.

Dunhuang Mogao Grottoes is a treasure of arts including architecture, painting and sculpture as well a treasure house of documents and cultural relics. The painting of Buddhist and other stories provide valuable materials for the study of China's ancient architecture as they describe many pavilions, temples, pagodas, palaces, courtyards, towns and bridges. The seated Buddha of colored clay smiles kindly, its brows curved and its mouth slightly upturned, reminding one of Leonardo da Vinci's Mona Lisa. Other paintings reproduce the communications and economic and cultural exchanges between China and foreign countries in musical, dancing performances and acrobatic shows. All of these provide pictorial evidence for the studies of the ancient Chinese society. It was one of China's most significant archaeological find. These precious relics are of great value to research of ancient Chinese politics, economy, culture and art, religion, science and nationalities, as well as friendly contacts between ancient China and foreign countries.

7 **Cultural Salon: Read the following passage, try to get some cultural knowledge about *Chinese painting and calligraphy* and answer following questions.**

Chinese painting has a high reputation throughout the world for its theory, expression, and techniques. It is a different art from Western painting. The painting is done using a brush on paper or silk, often with black ink alone. It is a monochromatic work of art derived from calligraphy. A Chinese painting is a distinctive object based on centuries-old traditions in China.

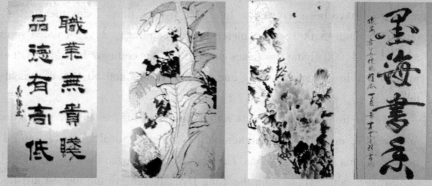

Chinese painting can be dated back to the Neolithic Period around 6,000 to 7,000 years old. It was closely related to crafts like colored potteries painted animals, fish, deer, birds, flowers, tree leaves, frogs and dancing people unearthed in the 1920's, which indicate that during the Neolithic Period Chinese had already begun to use brushes to paint. Paintings were mainly painted on a long and narrow piece of paper, silk or walls before the Tang Dynasty, and mural paintings were particularly popular.

Not like Western paintings, a Chinese painting is not restricted by the focal point in its perspective. Shifting perspective is one of the characteristics of Chinese painting. Chinese artists want to break the limitation of time and space to reflect the things which are far and near. The artists can use the shifting perspective to express freely what they want.

According to the techniques of expression, Chinese painting can be divided into two categories: the Xieyi school and the Gongbi school. The Xieyi painting is marked by exaggerated forms and freehand brush work. The Gongbi painting is the characterized by detail and fine brush work. A famous artist named Gu Kaizhi in the Jin Dynasty was the first person to put forward to the theory of "likeness in spirit resides in unlikeness" and "a painting should be something between likeness and unlikeness." In his opinion, a painting should express not only the appearance of an object, but also convey how the artist understands it. For example, the well-known modern painter named Qi Baishi doesn't paint shrimps as they are in nature; only their essence has been shown as a result of the artist's long-term observation and profound understanding.

Based on the themes of paintings, Chinese painting can be divided into three categories: landscapes, figures and birds-and-flowers. Landscapes and bird-and-flower paintings demonstrate the central place of nature in Chinese thought; figure paintings include the images of emperors, philosophers, and court ladies; religious paintings reflect both the Taoist philosophy native to China and Buddhism.

Figure painting was extended far beyond religious figures in the Song Dynasty (960—1127 A.D.). The art of figure painting was considered the golden age of in the Tang Dynasty (618—906 A.D.). Historical subjects and scenes of court life were common. Paintings of historical character and stories of daily life became extremely popular.

Landscape painting had already formed a unique style of expression by the 4th century. Gradually it was divided into two separate styles namely "blue-and-green" and "ink-and-wash" landscapes. The blue-and-green landscape used bright blue, green and red pigments derived from minerals to create a richly decorative style. The ink-and-wash landscape relied on vivid brushwork with varying degrees of intensity of ink to express the artist's conception of nature, his own emotions and individuality.

Flower-and-bird painting was separated from decorative art in the 9th century. Many well-known artists painted in this genre during the Song Dynasty and their themes included a variety of flowers, fruits, insects and fish. Many of the scholarly painters working with ink and brush illustrate plum blossoms, orchids, bamboo, chrysanthemums, pines and cypresses, which reflect their own ideals and character.

> Moreover, Chinese painting is a combination of the arts of poetry, calligraphy, painting and seal engraving. In ancient times most artists were poets and calligraphers. "Painting in poetry and poetry in painting" has been one of the criteria for excellent works. Inscriptions and seal impressions help to explain the artist's name, opinion and sentiments and also add decorative beauty to the painting.

1. What are the tools usually used in traditional Chinese painting?
_____

2. When can the Chinese painting be traced back?
_____

3. What are the characteristics of the traditional landscape painting?
_____

4. What are the features of the *"bird and flower"* painting?
_____

5. What else can you find on a masterpiece of traditional Chinese painting?
_____

■ Further reading: Introduction to Chinese Calligraphy

> Calligraphy is regarded as the art of writing beautiful handwriting with the brush, ink and paper or silk in China. Chinese calligraphy (Brush calligraphy) is a unique art to Asian cultures. In the history, Chinese calligraphy and Chinese Painting are closely related together, because calligraphy has always been held in equal importance to painting. Calligraphy and painting are the basic skills and disciplines of the Chinese literati. If you enter a study of scholar, four treasures of the study on the desk, such as writing brush, inkstick, inkstone and paper, are necessary.
>
> Chinese calligraphy is original from the hieroglyphs, in the process of evolution, it gradually has formed various styles and schools and become an important part of the heritage of national culture. Chinese calligraphy is generally divided into five forms: the seal character (zhuanshu), the official or clerical script (lishu), the regular script (kaishu), the running hand (xingshu) and the cursive hand (caoshu).
>
> 1) The zhuanshu (seal character) was the earliest form

of writing. This script is often used in seals, so it is also called the seal character, or the "curly script". When Emperor Qin Shihuang unified the whole country in 221 B.C., he ordered his Prime Minister Li Si to collect and sort out all the different systems of writing in different parts of the country. With a great effort, Emperor Qin Shihuang unified the written language and simplified the ancient zhuan script into small seal.

2) The lishu (official script) came in the wake of the xiaozhuan in the Qin Dynasty (221—207 B.C.). Although xiaozhuan is a simplified form of script, it was still too complicated for the scribes to copy increasing amount of documents. Cheng Miao, a prison warden, made a further simplification of the xiaozhuan, changing the curly strokes into straight and angular ones and thus making writing easier.

3) The kaishu (regular script) came into being in Wei Dynasty and developed in Jin Dynasty. The standard writing of the kaishu is square in form. If you want to become a calligrapher, you should start by learning to write kaishu, that is because the kaishu is based on a total eight kinds of strokes-the dot, the horizontal, the vertical, the hook, the rising, the left-falling and the right-falling and the bending strokes.

4) The caoshu (cursive hand) is used for making quick but rough copies. It is the characters are executed swiftly with the strokes running together. The characters are often joined up, with the last stroke of the first merging into the initial stroke of the next. They also change in size in the same piece of writing, all seemingly ordered by the whims of the writer. It is said that a calligrapher would not set about writing until he had got drunk. By the effect of alcohol, the calligrapher can make the brush to "gallop" across the paper, curling, twisting or meandering in one unbroken stroke.

5) The xingshu (running hand) is a kind of handwriting between the the kaishu and the caoshu. When carefully written with distinguishable strokes, the xingshu characters will be very close to the kaishu; when swiftly written, they will be similar with the caoshu. The best example for xingshu, all Chinese calligraphers will agree, is the Inscription on Lanting Pavilion written by the famous calligrapher—Wang Xizhi (321—379) in the Jin Dynasty, whose calligraphy has profoundly influenced on Chinese calligraphers and scholars in history.

To learn to write a nice handwriting in Chinese calligraphy, assiduous and persevering practice is necessary. Practice makes perfect, which is the motto by many great masters. During the imperial era, calligraphy was used as an important criterion for selection of executives to the imperial court. Unlike other visual art techniques, all calligraphy strokes are permanent, demanding careful planning and confident execution, which is the basic personalities required for an administrator. By controlling the concentration of ink, the thickness and absorbability of the paper, and the flexibility of the brush, the artist is free to produce an infinite variety of styles and forms. To the artist, calligraphy is a mental exercise that coordinates the mind and the body to choose the best styling in expressing the theme. It is also a most relaxing yet highly disciplined exercise indeed for one's body and mind.

8 Work in Pairs.

> **Student A** You are a European visitor to China.
>
> **Student B** You are a tour guide.
> Studest A asks Student B to introduce the Chinese calligraphy.

9 Supplementary task: Introduce one of Humane Landscapes you are interested in. Make a presentation in class. The teacher and students will comment on your presentation and the main points of the introduction to Humane Landscapes.

Unit 8 Religious Temples

AIMS

- To understand what and how to prepare for talking about Buddhist temples
- To find ways to improve your guiding skills and performance
- To master the basic words and expressions of talking about Buddhist temples
- To know some basic knowledge about Buddhism and understand the main features of Buddhist temples

Make a list of all the common words you know in introducing Buddhist temples.

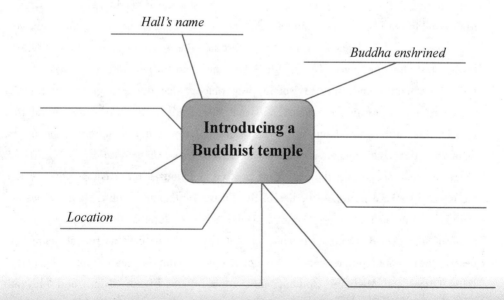

UNIT 8 RELIGIOUS TEMPLES

1 Read the following speech *Potala Temple in Tibet* and answer the questions.

Welcome to Lhasa for sightseeing. In this journey, we will appreciate the unique Tibet scenery and its outlandish culture, the world famous Potala Palace is our visiting place today.

Budala is Tibetan transliteration, namely Puto Luo, which means the place where bodhisattva lives. The Potala Palace is seated on the Mabu Mountain (Red Mountain) that locates in Lhasa city; it is not only a group of buildings involved the ancient architectural style of the palace, fort and temple together, but also the cultural treasure manifested the soul of the Tibetan Buddhism. The peak of the palace is 3767.19 m above sea level—the highest ancient palace in the world. In 1961, it was announced as the important cultural relic under state protection, in 1994, listed to the world cultural heritage ranks.

It was built to commemorate a historical fact. In 641, after marrying Princess Wencheng, Songtsen Gampo decided to build a grand palace to accommodate her and let his descendants remember the event. However, as a result of lightening strike and succeeding warfare during Landama's reign, the original palace was destroyed. In seventeenth century under the reign of the Fifth Dalai Lama, Potala was rebuilt, later; the Thirteenth Dalai Lama expanded it to today's scale. Potala Palace includes four major parts: the Red Palace and the White Palace on the Red Mountain, the Dragon King Pond to the back of the mountain and the "snow" area at the foot of the mountain.

The Red Palace locates on the center and also the apex of the entire construction. It was built after the death of the Fifth Dalai Lama and for generations it serves as the Dalai tope palace and Buddha worshipping place, also the symbol of the Buddha world and the center of the space. The Great West Hall is the hub of this grand Red Palace; the Fifth Dalai Lama's life is recorded here with fine murals, one of the extraordinarily vivid scenes is his visiting to Emperor Shunzhi in Beijing in 1652. There are four chapels in the hall. The west chapel houses three gold stupas, where the mummified and perfumed bodies of the Fifth, Tenth and Twelfth Dalai Lamas are well kept. Among the three, the Fifth Dalai Lama's stupa is the biggest, which is made of sandalwood, wrapped in gold foil and decorated with thousands of diamonds, pearls, agates and others gems. The north chapel contains statues of Sakyamuni, Dalai Lamas and Medicine Buddha, and stupas of the Eighth, Ninth and Eleventh Dalai Lamas'. Against the wall is Tanjur (The abhidharma division of the Tripitaka-Beijing edition),—the most important Tibetan Buddhist sutra sent to the Seventh Dalai Lama by Emperor Yongzheng. In the east chapel a two-meter high statue of

Tsong Khapa, the founder of Gelugpa Order, is enshrined and worshipped. In addition, about 70 famous adepts in Tibetan Buddhism surround him. In the south chapel, a silver statue of Padmasambhava, who is regarded by the Nyingmapa Order as their founder, and 8 bronze statues of his reincarnations are enshrined. On the floor above, there is a gallery which has a collection of 698 murals, portraying Buddhas, Bodhisattvas, Dalai Lamas, great adepts and narrating jataka stories (the sutra to narrate the birth stories of Shakyamuni in present life, past lives, and effects related to the past lives and the present life) and significant Tibetan historic occurrences. To the west of the Great West Hall locates the Thirteenth Dalai Lama's stupa hall. Since he was considered as great as the Fifth, people started to build his stupa after his death in the fall of 1933. Murals in the hall tell important events during his life, including his meeting with Emperor Guangxu.

Dharma Cave and the Saint's Chapel are the only survival structures built in the seventh century. They both lie in the center of the Red Palace. Inside the cave, statues of Songtsen Gampo, Princess Wencheng, Princess Tritsun and his chief ministers are enshrined. In the Saint's Chapel, Chenrezi, Tsong Khapa, Padmasambhava, the Fifth, Seventh, Eighth and Ninth Dalai Lamas are enshrined and worshipped. Visitors may find a footprint-stone that was believed left by the infant Twelfth Dalai Lama. The Red Palace was mainly used for religious service.

The White Palace usually serves for secular affairs—the political headquarter and Dalai Lamas' residence. Around the large and open courtyard, once there was a seminary and dormitories. The West Chamber of Sunshine and the East Chamber of Sunshine lie at the roof of the White Palace, where sun shines all day long, so get the names. They belonged to the Thirteenth and Fourteenth Dalai Lama respectively. Beneath the East Chamber of Sunshine is the largest hall in the White Palace, where Dalai Lamas ascended throne and ruled Tibet.

Dragon King Pond is the back garden of the Potala Palace, the dragon king palace and the elephant hall were built on the island in the center of the lake. The "snow" area—the jail of the Gaxag government, the room for printing sutra, the workshop and the horse stable, is under the Polata Palace foot. The periphery is the palace wall and the blockhouse. Standing at the foot of the Red Mountain, we can view the overall layout of the Palace, from bottom to top; they are"snow", the White Palace and the Red Palace. These three sections have symbolized the Tibetan Buddhist three-realm saying: the desire realm, the form realm and the formless realm. Through art presentation, the mighty heavenliness of the Buddhist world is displayed attractively. Thousand years later it still rouses our reverent emotion towards the heaven region.

UNIT 8 RELIGIOUS TEMPLES

> **VOCABULARY ASSISTANT**
>
> abhidharma 论藏
> desire realm 欲界
> Gelugpa Order 格鲁派
> Nyingmapa Order 宁玛派
> The Potala Palace 布达拉宫
> Padmasambhava 莲花生大士
> Red Palace 红宫
> realm 界
> secular 世俗
> Tsong Khapa 宗喀巴
> Tanjur《丹珠尔》(藏传佛教大藏经之《论藏》)
>
> dharma 达摩
> form realm 色界
> jataka 本生经
> periphery 外围
> Princess Wencheng 文成公主
> Princess Tritsun 尺尊公主(尼泊尔)
> reincarnation 化身
> reverent 虔诚的
> Songtsen Gampo 松赞干布
> White Palace 白宫

1. What should be involved when introducing a Buddhism temple?
   _____

2. How many parts does Potala Palace include?
   _____

3. What do the Red Palace and the White Palace serve for?
   _____

4. What are the three sections in the Tibetan Buddhism?
   _____

5. Who were the two greatest Dalai Lamas in history in your opinion?
   _____

2 **Fill in the gaps with a suitable word from the box. Change their forms if necessary.**

mural	overall layout	political headquarter	stupa
cultural heritage	three-realm	sandalwood	ascend
Red Palace	apex	survival	Dragon King Pond

1. Budala was listed as the important cultural relic under state protection, later affirmed as the world _____.
2. The Fifth Dalai Lama's life is recorded with fine _____.
3. The White Palace mainly serves as the _____ and Dalai Lamas' living quarters.
4. Dalai Lamas _____ throne and ruled Tibet in the White Palace.
5. We can view the _____ of the Palace at the foot of the Red Mountain.
6. These three sections have manifested the Tibetan Buddhism _____ saying.

7. The Fifth Dalai Lama's _____ is the biggest, which is made of _____, wrapped in gold foil.
8. The _____ was built after the death of the Fifth Dalai Lama, it locates on the center and also the _____ of the entire construction.
9. Dharma Cave and the Saint's Chapel are the only _____ structures built in the seventh century.
10. _____ is the back garden of the Potala Palace.

3 **Talk about the famous scenic spots or stories of Potala Temple in Tibet.**

People's religious feeling

Fifth Dalai Lama's stupa

Fifth Dalai Lama's visit of Emperor Shunzhi

Outlook of the Potala Temple

4 **Read the following passage and answer the questions.**

Wutai Mountain

Wutai Mountain is situated in the northeast part of Wutai county, Shanxi Province, with a total mountain area of about 250 sqkm around. It is the highest mountainous land in north China, so called "roof ridge of north China". The name Wutai comes from the mountain's natural shape, it has five main peaks with flat and broad platforms on each peak. Since the climate in the mountains is chilly, it's also named the Cool Mountain. Wutai Mountain is worldwide famous for its being looked up to as the Buddhist sacred land—one of the five main Buddhist holy lands in the world and ranks first among the four main Buddhist Mountains in China.

Mt. Wutai is identified as Manjusri's site of enlightenment; he is one of the Four Great Bodhisattvas, the one with the greatest wisdom, often placed on the left of Sakyamuni and always rides on a lion. Manjusri is the object for the believers' pilgrimage to Mt. Wutai. The temples on the mountain were initially built in the Han Dynasty, with the prosperity of Manjusri belief in Tang Dynasty, for a time the figures of temple increased up to 360 or so, but only 58 survived.

Wutai Mountain treasures many kinds of ancient architectures of China, from the Dynasty of the Tang, Song, Liao, Jin, Yuan, Ming, Qing to the Republic of China all left buildings of typical types and this itself is a valuable relic in Chinese architecture history. Hundreds of Buddha statues, stone tablets, scripture books, frescoes are well reserved. They make a worthy contribution to the study of the ancient Chinese civilization. Now we will introduce the main representative constructions.

XianTong temple, the leader temple in Wutai Mountain-the earliest, the oldest and the biggest, is situated at the south foot of LingJiu peak in the central district of Taihuai town, occupies a land of 12 mu and has 400 houses and 65 halls in total. Originally, it was built in the 11th year of Emperor Yongping, East Han Dynasty and has a history of nearly 2000 years, during the long period it had been rebuilt several times; the present constructions are the works of the Ming Dynasty and Qing Dynasty. Most sceneries and sites of Wutai Mountain are in and around this temple.

Dragon and Tiger Tablets

There are two stone tablets on either side of Xiantong Temple gate, the two Chinese characters "dragon and tiger" were carved on them respectively. They have the implied meaning that dragon and tiger are guarding the temple. The tablets are the rare relics of the Tang Dynasty.

Bell Tower

The Bell Tower is located in front of the temple. On the beam of this two-storeyed and three-eaved building hangs a bronze bell, which is the largest bell in Wutai Mountain, also called long ringing bell or long life bell. It was cast in July of the 48th year of Wanli period, the Ming Dynasty, with a weight of 9999.5 jin (to avoid the emperor's taboo figure of Wan-10 thousand). The bell sound can spread too far away, so it is always the symbol of the Buddhism ambience of Wutai Mountain.

Beamless Hall

The Beamless Hall in the temple is a complete-brick white building built only by laying up bricks without using of beams, so gets the name "beamless hall", looking outside it is quite European in style, white represents pureness in the west, while symbolizes the Buddhist pure land and boundless brightness here. A statue of Buddha of Immeasurable Life is worshipped here, so also called Wuliang Hall. The whole structure of the large hall is a miraculous view, it is a two-storeyed and 7-room hall looking externally, but only 3 rooms and one floor inside. This large hall was built in the 37th year of Wanli period, and has a history of nearly 400 years till now. The complete brick structure is one of the distinguished features of Xiantong Temple. Beamless Hall still has another name called "Seven-Site and Nine-Meeting Hall" which means Sakyamuni taught scriptures in seven places for nine times.

Daxiong Precious Hall—Hall of Sakyamuni

Another name of this hall is Large Buddha Hall, it is the main building in Xiantong Temple, occupies about 600 sqm. The particular feature of the hall is its complete wood-form frame, the whole rooftop is supported by columns only and the wall just served to shield off wind and resist cold. In the hall three worlds Buddha statues are worshipped, Shakyamuni Buddha in the middle, Amitabha Buddha in the west and Medicine Buddha in the east, 18 Arhat statues sit on each side. The place is also used for holding grand Buddhist activities.

Bronze Hall

The world-known Bronze Hall is established in the back part of Xiantong Temple. This 8.3m high, 4.7m wide and 4.5m deep hall was fully built with bronze of 10 thousand jin, 10 thousand statues of Buddhas were carved inside, therefore, also called ten-thousand-Buddha hall. Once there were five bronze pagodas in front of the hall, which implied the five platforms of Wutai Mountain, unfortunately only two survive today. Since this hall was made of complete bronze by casting, it forms another feature of Xiantong Temple—complete bronze structure.

Large Manjusri Hall

Wutai Mountain is the place where Manjusri makes Buddhist rites, so Wenshu Hall was built in most of the temples, while this hall was prefixed with a "large", and there contains several meanings: first, Xiantong Temple is the largest temple on Wutai Mountain; second, this temple has the largest floor area in all the temples of Wutai Mountain; third, seven Manjusri statues were worshipped here, the largest in number; this temple also remains as the most integrally preserved one in Wutai Mountain, so it is called the Large Manjusri Hall.

There are still many other enchanting sights on Wutai Mountain worth our seeing, the Large White Tower in Tayuan Temple—the symbolic building of Wutai Mountain, the Thousand Alms-bowl Manjusri Statue in the Thousand Alms-bowl Manjusri Hall, the Avatamsaka Sutra Scripture Tower displayed in the Sutra Holding Hall. As the world famous Buddhist sacred land, today Wutai Mountain has been attracting more and more pilgrims to pray for good fortune.

VOCABULARY ASSISTANT

ambience 气氛
Arhat 阿罗汉
fresco 壁画
Medicine Buddha 药师佛
site of enlightenment 道场
Avatamsaka Sutra 华严经
Buddha of Immeasurable Life 无量寿佛
Seven-Site and Nine-Meeting Hall 七处九会殿

Amitabha Buddha 阿弥陀佛
Bodhisattva 菩萨
Manjusri 文殊菩萨
pilgrimage 朝圣
scripture 经文
Shakyamuni Buddha 释迦牟尼佛

1. Why Wutai Mountain is also named the Cool Mountain?

2. What makes Wutai Mountain famous for?

3. Could you say something about Manjusri?

4. What kinds of ancient architectures does Wutai Mountain treasure?

5. What are the distinguished building features of Xiantong Temple in Wutai Mountain?

6. Why was the Beamless Hall also called Wuliang (无量) Hall?

7. Could you name some other sights in Wutai Mountain that not mentioned in the material?

8. Why Xian Tong Temple is the leader temple in Wutai Mountain?

9. How do you introduce Daxiong Precious Hall to the visitors?

10. Could you name the three Buddhas enshrined in the Hall of Sakyamuni?

5 Try to fill in the following chart about how to introduce Wutai Mountain to the guests.

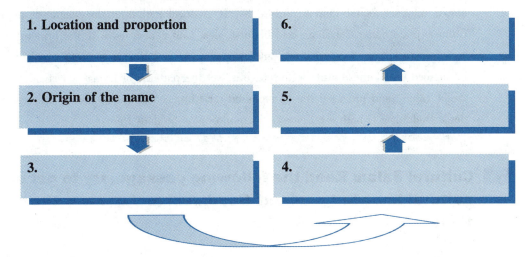

1. Location and proportion
2. Origin of the name
3.
4.
5.
6.

6 Rewrite the following passage into a dialogue and practice with your partners.

> As early as primitive society, religion already existed. The root of it is based on the lower level of productive development and people's weak force in struggling with the nature. From then on, for humans, whether as communities or individuals, religion has never been dismissed. In a sense, it can be looked as a partner of humans and is greeted in awe and never leaves.
>
> China is a multi-religious country. Religious believers mainly believe in Buddhism, Taoism, Islam, Catholicism and Christianity. Besides, some minorities have kept nature worship and multi-beliefs. Among them only Taoism originates from China natively, the others are all introduced from foreign countries in different history stages. Once entered into our country, they gradually formed the religious sects with Chinese characteristics for the influence of China's traditional culture.
>
> Chinese religion is an integral part of the whole of traditional Chinese culture. It plays a very important role as the new century begins, especially in the era initiated by the establishment of the people's republic of China.
>
> Confucianism is a special form of religion in China. Though some academic communities have different points of view about whether Confucianism is a religion or not. The long-time-existed Confucianism ruled Chinese thought and stabilized the feudal society for thousands of years, so to some degree, for its wide spread and deep influence it can also be regarded as a kind of religion in China. Han people are mostly affected by Confucianism, which in certain period of history is the main belief even,

while Buddhism and Taoism are secondary and others supplementary.

Every religious belief involves a religion and a philosophy. Confucianism has less actual religious belief than a philosophy. It is developed from the teachings of the Chinese philosopher Confucius and his disciples, and concerned with the principles of good conduct, practical wisdom, and proper social relationships. Confucianism has influenced the Chinese attitude toward life, set the patterns of living and standards of social value, and provided the background for Chinese political theories and institutions. Buddhism is both a religion and a philosophy. So does Daoism.

7 **Cultural Salon: Read the following passage, try to get some cultural knowledge about *Buddhism* and answer the questions.**

Buddhism was founded in India in the 6th century BC by Siddhatha Gautama, the son of King Suddhodhana (literally "pure rice") who governed the Indian state of Kapilavastu near the present borders of India and Nepal. He is titled Sakyamuni (the sage of the Sakya family). Legendarily speaking, one day he walked into the street from the palace and met the old, the sick, the poor and the corpses. These sights revealed to him another aspect of life he never lived as a prince, which deeply touched him and made him break from the material world and became an ascetic. But the ascetic experience didn't bring him what he expected, so six years later, he gave up such life. At last, after mystic concentration under a bodhi tree for seven days and nights, he became enlightened, then founded an order of mendicants and spent the next 45 years preaching his ideas until death.

The "four noble truths" preached by Sakyamuni are: first, the truth of suffering, which means affliction is the universal taste of mankind, and everybody is subject to the trauma of birth, of sickness, decrepitude and death; second, the truth of the arising of suffering, explaining the cause of suffering is desire, the desire for the objects and situations that can meet one's personal fulfillment; third, the truth of the cessation of suffering, means the stop of suffering can only be achieved by removing desire; fourth, the truth of the path to the cessation of suffering, which reveals that desire can be abandoned if one follows the right path. Then the correct (noble) eightfold path was taught by Sakyamuni, which remains one of the cornerstones of Buddhist practice.

These are: (1) right view, the correct knowledge about life but from the Buddhist point of understanding; (2) right thought, the correct thought about what life's problems are; (3) right speech, this item is to let one avoid lies, idle talk, abuse, slander and deceit; (4) right action, to show kindness and avoid self-seeking in all behaviors. It also includes five rules: no killing; no stealing; no improper sexual action; no false speech; no consumption of alcohol; (5) right livelihood, which asks one to engage a suitable activity to earn a living; (6) right effort, the will to develop virtues and to curb passions; (7) right mindfulness, one is asked to be removed from evil thought, be mindful of the Buddha-way, be mindful of reality and not to be taken in by appearances; (8) right concentration, it is the way to Enlightenment through maintenance of unscattered mindfulness in formal meditation. By following the noble eightfold path, one can become Buddha and attain nirvana, a state of bliss, ecstasy. The four noble truths and the correct eightfold path form the main content of the Buddha's first sermon. Buddhism has survived by adapting and re-inventing itself in different aspects, not by holding on to old ideologies and rituals. With time going, its contents can be improved to meet the need of social development.

There are two main schools in Buddhism, Mahayana Buddhism (Great Vehicle or Bodhisattva Vehicle) and Hinayana (Small Vehicle or Liberated Vehicle) Buddhism.

Mahayana Buddhism is popular in China, Korea, Japan, Mongolia, Tibet and other places in the Far East. It is also called Northern Buddhism. The true intention of the Buddha in Mahayana is not simply to rescue sentient beings, who, once saved, play a secondary and subservient role; rather, it is to help sentient beings attain Enlightenment and Buddhahood, that is to become equal to the Buddhas in all sides. This is a unique and revolutionary feature of Buddhism. It is called the Great Vehicle because its teachings are like a vast wagon capable of carrying many to release from rebirth. This sect emphasizes the existence of many Buddhas-the Buddhas in heaven and people-to-be Buddhas in the future.

Mahayana Buddhism plays an important part in various fields in China. It brought to Chinese literature new conceptions, literary styles, and techniques of word-building in language. Buddhist painting and sculpture have left a rich source of material for the study of Chinese art and history, which highlight a brilliant chapter in China's cultural history. China's music, astronomy, medicine, and gymnastics all reflect the influences of the Mahayana Buddhism.

Hinayana is popular in Sri Lanka, Burma, Thailand, and some ethnic minorities in Yunnan Province, known as Southern Buddhism. This sect strives to become an

Arhat, a person who has single-heartedly overcome his passions and ego, thereby gaining liberation for himself. Because of its emphasis on individual self-liberation, it is known in northern Buddhist countries somewhat disparagingly as the Lesser Vehicle. Hinayana Buddhism claims Buddha as a historical figure, while Mahayana believes Sakyamuni a superman. This sect keeps the monastic life as virtue and the Tripitaka as authority. To some extent, Hinayana Buddhism is much closer in tenet to the original teaching of Buddha.

OCABULARY ASSISTANT

Siddhatha Gautama 乔达摩·悉达多　　King Suddhodhana 净饭王
Kapilavastu 迦毗罗卫国　　　　　　　mystic concentration 禅定
four noble truths 四圣谛　　　　　　　truth of suffering 苦谛
arising of suffering 集谛　　　　　　　cessation of suffering 灭谛
path to the cessation of suffering 道谛　　eightfold path 八圣道
Tripitaka 三藏

1. What made Sakyamuni give up the life of a prince?

2. What are the four noble truths and the correct eightfold path?

3. What are the two sects of Buddhism?

4. How does Buddhism influence our life, especially Mahayana Buddhism?

5. What are the main characteristics of Hinayana Buddhism?

Further reading: Taoism

Taoism is the only native-born religion in China, before it turned to be a religion, Taoist thought had already existed, it is the fruit of our traditional culture and has close connection with many fields of ancient Chinese conventions, such as witchcraft, rules of immortality, ancestor worship and Taoist philosophy. Strictly speaking, as a religious organization, Taoism was founded at the end of Eastern Han Dynasty by Zhang Daoling, and gained its official status during Tang Dynasty. The believers look up to Laozi as their supreme god, and take Dao De Jing as canon. Dao De Jing is an extensive and profound book, the idea of non-action runs through all the content, which is also the central tenet of Taoism.

Taoism takes "Dao" as their uppermost belief, the word "Dao" means "the way", it is formless but all the things in the universe come into being from it. Following this way, man acts without action, does without doing, so greatness can be achieved. Taoists believe in immortality, so cultivating themselves and being immortal is their ultimate destination. One way of gaining an ever-living body was to eat elixir, so alchemy was developed, which makes a great contribution to our science, though none reached immortality by using such "medicine".

Taoism emphasizes the union of man and nature, preaching the points that the world itself is a fullness existence, one touch of improving will destroy its perfectness. Yin and Yang are two polar opposites into which all elements can be classified, male and female, strong and weak, soft and hard, life and death are the presentation of this two elementary powers, they function by reciprocal movement and make the whole universe a harmonious unity. Taoists always use the image of water to represent their antilogy: nothing under heaven is softer or more yielding than water, but it can overcome the hardest. They want to prove that the yielding conquers the resistant and the soft conquers the hard is a dead fact.

Various schools of Taoism appeared in different stages in Chinese history, for years of reform and improvement, at last they emerged into two major sects: the True Unity Sect founded by Zhang Daoling and the Complete Unity Sect founded by Wang Chongyang.

As an indispensable part of Taoist culture, famous Taoist mountains are attracting more and more tourists to pay their visit, such as Qingcheng Mountain in Sichuan Province, Wudang Mountain in Hubei Province and Sanqing Mountain in Jiangxi Province. What impresses us most in traveling is the Taoist temples, most of them were situated in bright and fresh natural conditions and left us both scenic spots for visiting and cultural relics for studying. Some well-known Taoist temples are Beijing Baiyun Temple, which is the holy land for the Complete Unity Sect and the center of North Taoism, Louguantai Temple in Shanxi Province, which is regarded as the birthplace of Taoism, Xuanmiao Temple in Jiangsu Province, Chongxu Temple in Luofu Mountain, Guangdong Province. Besides these well-known ones there are still many temples in local places.

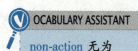

VOCABULARY ASSISTANT

non-action 无为   alchemy 炼金术
True Unity Sect 正一道   Complete Unity Sect 全真教

8 Work in Pairs.

Student A You are a European visitor to China.

Student B You are a tour guide.
Student A asks Student B to introduce the main schools of Buddhism.

9 Supplementary task: Introduce a Buddhist temple you are interested in or talk about a famous mountain related to Buddhism. Make a presentation within ten minutes in class. The teacher and students will make comments on what you tell.

Unit 9 Natural Landscapes

AIMS

- To understand how to introduce a city with natural landscapes
- To grasp the special characteristics of different cities
- To master the basic words and expressions of talking about natural landscapes
- To try to explain the typical sceneries in these cities

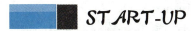# START-UP

Make a list of all the common words you know about a beautiful natural landscape.

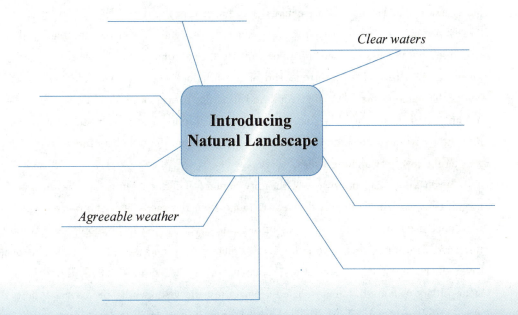

1 Read the following speech *Guilin* and answer the questions.

Ladies and Gentlemen, welcome to Guilin. It is situated in the northeast of Guangxi Zhuang Autonomous Region and on the west bank of the Lijiang River, Guilin is a beautiful city with a history of around 2000 years.

Guilin features the subtropical monsoon climate with an agreeable weather and plenty of rain. The average temperature of Guilin is about 18℃ with the lowest down to 8℃ in the coldest day of the winter and up to no more than 28℃ in the hottest day of the summer. That's the reason why you can visit Guilin all the year round and of course in Guilin, there is no low tourist season. Famed for scenery unparalleled in China's vast land, Guilin has its unique and picturesque landscape reputed as green hills, clear waters, fantastic caves and pretty rocks. Hills in Guilin thrust into the heaven with the Lijiang River twists and turns with them. The geological study has it that Guilin area belongs to the Karst formation. About 300 million years ago, here used to be a vast ocean. The upheaval movement of the earth crust sent the limestone on the sea-bed up above the water, which exposed, weathered and eroded for long time in the air has become forests of peaks of fantastic shapes, labyrinths of dissolved caves and marvelous rivers under the ground. Thus a unique and picturesque landscape in Guilin occurred.

The oddly-shaped hills rising out of flat ground, in various shapes resemble buns, saw-tooth, bamboo shoot, camels, etc. Located at the riverside of Lijiang River, the Elephant Trunk Hill is shaped very much like a giant elephant standing by the riverside, gulping water from the river with its trunk dipping into it. It was formerly known as Li Hill and because one end of the hill looks like the elephant trunk, so comes the name of the Elephant Trunk and it is also a symbol of Guilin city. There is not only a good view of hills, but also rivers. The Lijiang River is crystal clear, and no matter how deep the water is, you can see the bottom-the pebbles, sand, weeds as well as the lovely swimming fishes.

Seven kilometers northwest of the city center, the Reed Flute Cave is the most magnificent cave in Guilin. It derives its name from the reeds at its entrance, which were once used to make flutes. It was in the Tang Dynasty that local people discovered this cave. The huge karst cave is about 500 meters deep and 240 meters wide. In the cave, there are a lot of stalactites, stalagmites, stone screens, stone flowers and stone pillars of fantastic shapes. They seem to tell the visitors why the cave is known also as a place of natural art. Their shapes suggest images of old trees, dense shrubs, ferocious beasts and human figures. Especially the vast grotto, known as the crystal palace, is capable of holding some 1000 people. Legend has it that a peculiar stone pillar in the grotto is the Dragon King's magic needle. Tourists from home and abroad compare this cave to the art gallery of nature.

A visit to Guilin is not complete without a boat excursion down the Lijiang River to Yangshuo, about 83 km from Guilin city. The tourists must be attracted by the picturesque sceneries on both banks of the river. As everyone knows, "Guilin has the most beautiful scenery in China, and Yangshuo is the most beautiful part of Guilin."

VOCABULARY ASSISTANT

subtropical monsoon 亚热带季风	agreeable 宜人的
unparallel 不平行的	picturesque 景色如画的
thrust 插入	Karst formation 喀斯特地貌
limestone 石灰石	erode 侵蚀；腐蚀
labyrinth 迷宫	the Elephant Trunk Hill 象鼻山
gulp 吞咽,饮	pebble 鹅卵石
the Reed Flute Cave 芦笛洞	stalactite 钟乳石
stalagmite 石笋	ferocious 凶猛的
grotto 洞穴	excursion 游览,参观

1. Where is Guilin situated?

2. Why is it said that there is no low tourist season in Guilin?

3. What are the main sceneries in Guilin? Try to tell their features in detail.

4. Try to explain what karst formation is?

5. Which is the most beautiful part of Guilin?

2 Fill in the gaps with a suitable word from the box. Change their forms if necessary.

situate	city center	excursion	Reed Flute Cave
Dragon King's	Karst	subtropical	Elephant Trunk Hill
average	scenery		

1. Guilin is _____ in the northeast of Guangxi Zhuang Autonomous Region.
2. Guilin features the _____ monsoon climate.
3. The _____ temperature of Guilin is about 18℃.
4. The geological study has it that Guilin area belongs to the _____ formation.

5. Located at the riverside of Lijiang River, the _____ is shaped very much like a giant elephant standing by the riverside.
6. Seven kilometers northwest of the _____, the Reed Flute Cave is the most magnificent cave in Guilin.
7. Legend has it that a peculiar stone pillar in the grotto is the _____ magic needle.
8. A visit to Guilin is not complete without a boat _____ down the Lijiang River to Yangshuo.
9. The _____ is about 500 meters deep and 240 meters wide.
10. Guilin has the most beautiful _____ in China, and Yangshuo is the most beautiful part of Guilin.

3 **Talk about the famous scenic spots in Guilin.**

the Elephant Trunk Hill

the Reed Flute Cave

Lijiang River

Karst formation

4 **Read the following passage and answer the questions.**

Sanya, Xiamen and Dalian

Sanya is a world-famous coastal tourism city with tropical landscapes and special local customs. Located on the southern tip of Hainan Island, Sanya stands almost the same latitude as Hawaii. Thus, it's often called "the Hawaii of China" or "orient Hawaii".

The area of Sanya is about 1,919 square kilometers, 91.6 kilometers long from the east to the west, and 51.2 kilometers wide from the north to the south. And the coastline is about 209.1 kilometers. The beaches are the biggest attraction. Sanya has some of the most beautiful and well maintained stretches of sand not only in China but also in southern Asia. The sand here is white, palm trees provide shelter from the sun and the sea is wonderfully blue and warm. This is maybe the only place in China with a really laid-back feeling and atmosphere.

Its tourist attractions include Yalong Bay National Holiday Resort, Dadonghai Tourist Zone, TianyaHaijiao, Luhuitou Park, Nanshan Cultural and Tourist Zone, the marvelous landscape of mountains and seas at Nanshan, Wuzhizhou Island, the Ancient City of Yazhou, Shuinan Village, Luobidong Cavern and the Muslim tombs built in Tang & Song dynasties, etc. Local specialties include handicrafts made of seashells, horn-ware, coconut shell carving products, squid and pepper, etc.

Well, let's turn to another seashore city—Xiamen, which is called Amoy in the past. As a major seaport since ancient times, Xiamen boasts a wide gulf with deep water but without freezing and silting. The name of "Xiamen" was consequently given, which means "a gate of China" and it's one of China's four earliest special economic zones. The city of Xiamen is a beautiful seaside garden, with islands, rock formations, temples, forests, cliffs, and flowers all competing with each other for attention. The local culture, Taiwanese customs, delicious seafood, and exotic architecture mix to form a truly charming city. Different from Sanya, it has a subtropical monsoon climate, it is spring all year round. Because of its unpolluted environment and wonderful natural landscape, Xiamen has been nationally accredited as a Sanitary City, Model City for Environmental Protection, Garden City, and Excellence in Tourism City. It is generally acknowledged as one of the most livable cities in China and is commonly described as "a city on the sea and sea in the city".

There are five main tourist areas in Xiamen which divided by old landscapes and developing new sceneries,—Gulangyu Island Tourist Area, Nanputuo Temple Tourist Area, Wanshi Rock Tourist Area, Huangcuo Tourist Area and Jimei Tourist Area. Gulangyu Island is a pearl shining in the Xiamen Harbor. It is famous for the attractive architecture and for having China's largest piano museum. We call it the piano island because people here love to play the piano. They have about 600 pianos in this islet, though there is only a population of 20,000 people. The architecture in the island has various styles, Chinese and foreign, therefore it is also called "the World Architecture Museum". The air in the islet is fresh. You cannot see any sorts of vehicles and is pretty quiet. All these render an atmosphere of a fairyland. Sunlight Rock is the symbol of Xiamen. With the height of 93 meters, it is the highest peak in Gulangyu Island. Overlooking the island from here, red housetops, green plants, blue sea and the modern buildings make a beautiful view.

Talking about the well-known seaside cities in China, we cannot ignore Dalian, a city full of magic. To some extent it is one of the most beautiful and romantic city of China. Bordered by the Bohai Sea and the Yellow Sea, Dalian is situated at the southern end of the Liaodong Peninsula in northeastern China. This is a warm temperate zone with a semi-moist monsoon climate and ocean climate features. The sunny beach and clearly demarcated seasons make it the pleasant resort in summer. Being the largest ice-free harbor in the Northeast China, it is also a trading and financial center in northeastern Asia and has gained the name the "Hong Kong of Northern China".

People in Dalian have passions in fashion and sports. Dalian International Fashion Festival is held annually in autumn and makes the city into an ocean of beauty and joy. Dalian football team proves to be the best by winning most of the champion titles in the annual soccer league games in China.

There is a 32-kilometer-long road, from northeast to southwest, known as Binhai in Dalian. This coastal area is an ideal beach for the vacationers. The famous scenic spots of Bangchuidao Scenic Area, Laohutan Scenic Area, Jinshitan Scenic Area and Xinghai Square are spread around this region. Situated in the central part of the southern seashore of Dalian City, Laohutan Ocean Park is the biggest modern lido in China with a total area of 1,180,000 square meters and a coastline of more than 4 kilometers. In the Park, many attractive natural sceneries and magnificent man-made sights can be seen, especially the Tigers Sculpture Square and Laohutan Polar Region Marine Animals World. Xinghai Square situated in the beautiful Xinghai gulf, and thus the name from it. The total area of Xinghai square is 1.1 million square meters. It's the largest city square in Asia.

In addition to the stunning cliffs and scenic parks, numerous places along the coastline are good for beach resort visitors and water sports lovers. Meanwhile, you can taste the authentic Dalian-style seafood in a fisherman's house at an incredibly low price.

OCABULARY ASSISTANT

tropical 热带的
Yalong Bay 亚龙湾
TianyaHaijiao 天涯海角
Nanshan 南山
Yazhou 崖州
Luobidong 落笔洞

laid-back 松弛的，自在的
Dadonghai 大东海
Luhuitou 鹿回头
Wuzhizhou 蜈支洲
Shuinan 水南
squid 鱿鱼

Gulangyu 鼓浪屿	Nanputuo 南普陀
Wanshi Rock 万石岩	Huangcuo 黄厝
Jimei 集美	silt 淤沙
special economic zones 经济特区	exotic 异国情调的
subtropical monsoon 亚热带季风	to some extent 在某种程度上
peninsula 半岛	a warm temperate zone 暖温带
a semi-moist monsoon 半湿润季风	demarcated seasons 四季分明
passion 热情	soccer league games 足球联赛
Binhai 滨海	Bangchuidao 棒槌岛
Laohutan 老虎滩	Jinshitan 金石滩
Xinghai 星海	lido 海滨浴场
authentic 正宗的	
the World Architecture Museum 万国建筑博物馆	

1. Describe the different climate types of Sanya, Xiamen and Dalian.

_____

2. Why is Sanya often called "orient Hawaii"?

_____

3. What color is the sand in Sanya? Is it popular in China or Asia?

_____

4. What are the tourist attractions in Sanya?

_____

5. What has Xiamen been nationally accredited as?

_____

6. Why is Gulangyu Island called a piano island?

_____

7. How many main tourist areas are there in Xiamen? What are they?

_____

8. Explain the location of Dalian.

_____

9. What are the two things that have earned Dalian a great reputation?

_____

10. Say something about the famous scenic spots in Dalian.

_____

108 UNIT 9 NATURAL LANDSCAPES

5 Try to fill in the following chart about how to introduce a city to the guests.

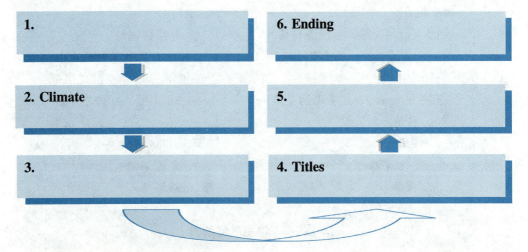

1.
2. Climate
3.
4. Titles
5.
6. Ending

6 Rewrite the following passage into a dialogue and practice with your partners.

Inner Mongolia Grassland

What is the most attractive about Inner Mongolia is its natural beauty. Vast grasslands, including the Hulunbeier Grassland, Gegentala Grassland and Huitengxile Grassland are all good places for a grassland experience. The Mongolian nationality is the dominant ethic group, and 35 other nationalities, such as Dawoer, Ewenke, Elunchun, Han, Manchu, Russian, etc. live in harmony with them on the grassland. The grassland looks like a soft, green carpet, the mushroom-like yurts, bright sky, fresh air, rolling grass and the flocks and herds moving like white clouds on the remote grassland, all contribute to make the scenery a very relaxing one. You can see numerous kinds of wild flowers coming out in summer, and wisps of smoke are rising continuously from the yurts scattered on the grassland. While visiting Inner Mongolia you may try different activities such as Mongolian wrestling, horse & camel riding, rodeo competitions, archery, visiting traditional families and enjoying the graceful Mongolian singing and dancing.

The best time to visit the grassland is definitely during the traditional Mongolian Nadamu Festival period when there is a better chance to both participate and feel the lively atmosphere of the grassland life. "Nadamu" in the Mongolian language means recreation and game, it is often held every July and August When it comes, there will be a lot of performances, such as horse racing, wrestling, archery and some other special ethnic activities. People use the Nadamu to celebrate good harvests and their good life. During that period, herdsmen often take the opportunity to sell domestic animals and livestock products and purchase daily necessities and livelihood-related goods. Actually, the herdsmen have few chances to get together on such vast grassland, so Nadamu also plays the role of a big trade fair for them.

The most common and grand sacrificial activity of the Mongolians is the sacrificing of Aobao. Aobao is a kind of altar or shrine made of a pile of stone, adobe bricks, and straw. Aobao is normally set up in hills and mountains, it is a cone-shaped solid tower made of stone. A long pole is inserted on the top, fur or animal skin and cloth ribbons are tied on the pole end, rocks for incense are placed around.

Sacrificing of Aobao is mostly held in June, July and August. When sacrificing, the worshipper will take Hadas, mutton, fermented milk and dairy food to the Aobao. Hadas and sacrifices will be presented firstly and Lamas will chant Buddhist scriptures and the other people will worship on bended knees. Then, they will add stone or wicker to the Aobao and colorful silk strips and Sutra streamers. After the sacrifice, such activities as horse races, wrestling and archery will be held; the event later will develop into a Nadamu meeting.

VOCABULARY ASSISTANT

Hulunbeier 呼伦贝尔	Gegentala 格根塔拉
Huitengxile 辉腾锡勒	dominant 占主要地位的
Dawoer 达斡尔	Ewenke 鄂温克
Elunchun 鄂伦春	ethic group 种群
yurt 蒙古包	flock 一群(羊)
herd 牧人	scatter 散落,分散
wrestle 摔跤	rodeo 马术比赛
archery 射箭	Nadamu 那达慕
ethnic 传统的,民族的	sacrificial 祭祀的
altar 祭坛	shrine 圣地,神祠
incense 香	Hada 哈达
mutton 羊肉	fermented 发酵的
scripture 经文	wicker 柳条

7 **Cultural Salon: Read the following passage, try to get some cultural knowledge about *Chinese Yin and Yang theory and Acupuncture* and answer the questions.**

Traditional Chinese medicine incorporates the *Yin* and *Yang* theory and the theory of the five elements (metal, wood, water, fire, and the earth), The former theory holds that the human body's life is the result of the balance of *Yin* and *Yang*. *Yin* is the inner and negative principles, and *Yang* is the outer and positive. The key reason why there is sickness is because the two aspects lose their harmony. When you feel tired or weak, maybe you have too much *Yin*, you should eat hot *Yang* foods, such as beef. But people who are too stressed out and angry may have too much *Yang*, Chinese doctors suggest them to eat more *Yin* foods like tofu. The latter theory believes that things in the universe are composed of five indispensable elements of daily life, which move and change constantly to promote and restrain each other.

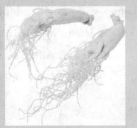  

Acupuncture is the insertion of very fine needles, (sometimes in conjunction with electrical stimulus), on the body's surface, in order to influence physiological functioning of the body.

As the basis of Acupuncture, Shen Nong theorized that the body had an energy force running throughout it. This energy force is known as Qi (roughly pronounced Chee). The Qi consists of all essential life activities which include the spiritual, emotional, mental and the physical aspects of life. A person's health is influenced by the flow of Qi in the body, in combination with the universal forces of *Yin* and *Yang*. *Yin* and *Yang* is an important theory in the discussion of Acupuncture treatment, in relation to the Chinese theory of body systems. As stated earlier Qi is an energy force that runs throughout the body. In addition, Qi is also prevalent throughout nature as well. Qi is comprised of two parts, *Yin* and *Yang*. *Yin* and *Yang* are opposite forces, that when balanced, work together. Any upset in the balance will result in natural calamities, in nature; and disease in humans. *Yin* is signified by female attributes, passive, dark, cold, moist, that which moves medially, and deficient of *Yang*. *Yang* is signified by male attributes, light, active, warm, dry, that which moves laterally, and deficient of *Yin*. Nothing is completely *Yin* or *Yang*. The most striking example of this is man himself. A man is the combination of his mother (*Yin*) and his father (*Yang*). He contains qualities of both: This is the universal symbol describing the constant flow of yin and yang forces. You'll notice that within yin, there is **Yang**, and within **Yang**, there is the genesis of **Yin**. Whether or not you believe in Taoist philosophy, (which all this is based on), one thing is indisputable: Acupuncture works.

Acupuncturists can use as many as nine types of Acupuncture needles, though only six are commonly used today. These needles vary in length, width of shaft, and shape of head. Today, most needles are disposable. They are used once and discarded in accordance with medical biohazard regulations and guidelines. There are a few different precise methods by which Acupuncturists insert needles. Points can be needled anywhere in the range of 15 degrees to 90 degrees relative to the skin surface, depending on the treatment called for. In most cases, a sensation, felt by the patient, is desired. This sensation, which is not pain, is called deqi (得气). The following techniques are some which may be used by an Acupuncturist immediately following insertion: Raising and Thrusting, Twirling or Rotation, Combination of Raising/Thrusting and Rotation, Plucking, Scraping (vibrations sent through the needle), and Trembling (another vibration technique). Once again, techniques are carefully chosen based on the ailment.

1. What do you know about Chinese medicine?

2. What is **Yin** and **Yang** according to Chinese medicine? And what are five elements?

3. What kind of food should a person eat when they feel uneasy and nervous?

4. What is acupuncture?

5. Do you think we should develop the Chinese medicine as before?

Further reading: Four Methods of Diagnosis

It is a wonder that Chinese doctors could cure countless patients without any assistant apparatus but only a physical examination. The four methods of diagnosis consist of observation, auscultation and olfaction, interrogation, pulse taking and palpation.

Observation indicates that doctors directly watch the outward appearance to know a patient's condition. As the exterior and interior corresponds immediately, when the inner organs run wrongly, it will be reflected through skin pallor, tongue, the facial sensory organs and some excrement.

Auscultation and olfaction is a way for doctors to collect messages through hearing the sound and smelling the odor. This is another reference for diagnosis.

Interrogation suggests that doctors question the patient and his relatives, so as to know the symptoms, evolution of the disease and previous treatments.

The taking of the pulse and palpation refer that doctors noting the pulse condition of patients on the radial artery, and then to know the inner change of symptom. Doctors believe that when the organic function is normal, the pulse, frequency, and intension of pulse will be relatively stable, and when not, variant.

When treating a disease, doctors of traditional Chinese medicine usually find the patient's condition through these four diagnostic methods: observation, auscultation and olfaction, interrogation, pulse, and palpation. Combining the collected facts and according to their internal relations, doctors will utilize the dialectics to analyze the source and virtue of the disease. Then make sure what prescription should be given. In traditional Chinese medical science, the drugs are also different from the West, because doctors have discovered the medicinal effects of thousand of herbs over a long period of time. Before taking the medicine, the patient will have to boil it. Then there is the distinctive method of preparation, associated with the acupuncture and massage, the treatment will take effect magically.

Such a complicated medical science had come down thanks to records like The Yellow Emperor's Canon of Interior Medicine, Shen Nong's Canon of Herbs, and the Compendium of Materia Medica, which are all comprehensive and profound works. There are also widespread stories praising the experienced and notable doctors in ancient China like Hua Tuo in the Three Kingdoms Periods (220—280). Today, though western medicine has been adopted, traditional treatments are still playing an important role and have raised great attention and interest worldwide due to the amazing curative effects reported.

8 Work in Pairs.

Student A You are a patient.

Student B You are a Chinese doctor.
Student A asks Student B to introduce the Chinese medicine.

9 Supplementary task: Introduce one kind of natural landscapes you are interested in or talk about Chinese Medicine. Make a presentation in ten minutes in class. The teacher and students will comment on what you say and check if you address the main points about the introduction.

Unit 10

Seeing-off the Guests

AIMS

- To understand how to introduce a city with natural landscapes
- To grasp the special characteristics of different cities
- To master the basic words and expressions of talking about natural landscapes
- To try to explain the typical sceneries in these cities

 START-UP

Make a list of all the common words you know in introducing arts and crafts.

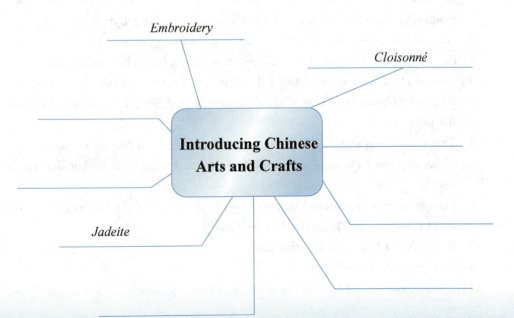

1 Read the following conversation and answer the questions.

At the Souvenir Shop

S: Shop Assistant   T: Tourist   L: Local Guide

T: Good morning. I'd like to buy some products of Chinese arts and crafts home. But I don't know what to buy. What do you recommend?

L: Good morning. Well. There are wide selection of articles in China, such as embroidery, pottery, cloisonné, metalwork, lacquerware, jade carving, furniture design, ivory carving, and textiles. All of them are typical Chinese arts and crafts. Shall we go to the biggest souvenir store after morning sightseeing?

T: I could not wait any longer. How about now?

L: There are two more tourists in our group, I'm afraid that we can not change our itinerary now. I promise that I'll show you there as soon as we finish the morning sightseeing.

S: Good morning, ma'am. What can I do for you?

T: I'm looking for some beautiful Chinese arts and crafts. Would you show me some?

S: Certainly. We have a great variety of them in our shop. How about the cloisonné? It is typical Chinese.

L: In China, the art of cloisonné is called Jingtai Blue, because the craftsmanship reached its highest level in the reign of Jingtai in the Ming Dynasty.

T: Ok. I'd like to buy some cloisonné vase to decorate my guestroom.

S: Do you like this medium-sized cloisonné vase with a light blue background?

T: Gorgeous! I think my husband will like it very much! How much dose it cost?

S: It costs 350 Yuan. Our shop holds a one-price policy. We are not allowed to change the price at will.

T: That sounds reasonable. I'll take a pair of them. And I'd like to buy another pair of medium-sized cloisonné vase with flowers and birds as the background for my sister.

L: Peony flower is the national flower of China. Do you like the one with the design of a Chinese ancient beauty and peony flower?

T: Well, shall I have a look at this vase?

S: With pleasure. Here you are.

T: It is extremely beautiful. This is the right gift for my sister. I'll take a pair of them too.

S: Shall I wrap them together or separately?

T: Separately, please. Can you mail them to London for me?

S: Sure, please write down your name and address on this slip.

T: Thank you. How much do I owe you then?

S: 1450 Yuan altogether, including the postage.
L: Shall we go for lunch after your payment?
T: Oh, wait a moment. Let's have a look at that counter. My friend wants me to buy some silk fabrics with traditional Chinese pattern for her.
S: What about silk garments? They are embroidered with dragons, pandas or phoenix, butterfly.
T: Can you show me some? Is it made of pure Chinese silk?
S: Sure, it is figured satin of natural silk. China is the cradle of silk fabrics. Which color would you like to have, dark or light?
T: I like light colors. I think the pink garment is quite good. Can I have a look?
S: Yes, madam. Here you are.
T: How much does it cost? And how can I wash it?
S: 450 Yuan. You can only wash it in lukewarm water. Don't rub and wring it.
T: It's a lot of money, but it looks beautiful, I'll take it. Can I pay by Visa Card?
S: We don't accept Visa, please pay in cash.
T: OK. Could you wrap it up for me?
S: Sure, Please keep this invoice well. You'll need it when you go through the Customs.
T: You are so kind, thanks a lot.

VOCABULARY ASSISTANT

cloisonne 景泰蓝制的,景泰蓝瓷器
lacquerware [总称]漆器
textile 纺织品,纺织的
gorgeous 华丽的,灿烂的
invoice 发票,发货单,货物

metalwork 金属制品,金属制造
ivory 象牙
typical 典型的,象征性的
satin 缎子,假缎,缎纹

1. According to your understanding, what is your option about "Shopping should be balanced with sightseeing"?

2. If a guest persists to buy antiques from a native people, what should the tour guide do?

3. What will be the best answer when a tourist asks whether he can buy something either in department store or private store?

4. What should the guide remind the tourists at a very large souvenir store?

5. What are the typical arts and crafts of China?

2. Fill in the gaps with a suitable word from the box. Change their forms if necessary.

| hold | reign | lukewarm | fabric | variety |
| look for | wrap | cash | invoice | mail |

1. I'm _____ some beautiful Chinese arts and crafts.
2. Can you _____ them to London for me?
3. You can only wash it in _____ water.
4. The art of cloisonné is called Jingtai Blue, because the craftsmanship reached its highest level in the _____ of Jingtai in the Ming Dynasty.
5. Our shop _____ a one-price policy.
6. My friend wants me to buy some silk _____ with traditional Chinese pattern for her.
7. We have a great _____ of them in our shop.
8. We don't accept Visa, please pay in _____.
9. Shall I _____ them together or separately?
10. You'll need _____ when you go through the Customs.

3. Talk about the history of Chinese arts and crafts.

Lacquer Wares

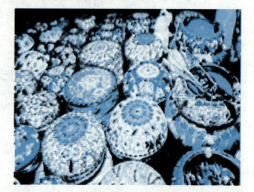
Cloisonné

Jade Objects

Porcelain

4 **Read the following dialogue and answer the questions.**

Seeing-off Tourists at the Airport

G: Local Guide   A: Tourist A   B: Tourist B

(*Li Lin, the local tour guide from Shanghai International Travel Service, is seeing two foreign tourists off at the airport*)

G: Excuse me. Have you double checked your passport, ticket, flight schedule and luggage?

A: Sure, I have double checked everything and put them in the car before we leave for the airport.

B: It's 10:30 a.m. now. We are two hours ahead the departure time.

G: Here we are. Don't leave your personal belongings behind! Let me handle your luggage.

B: Thanks. That's very kind of you. I am afraid I have to buy the departure tax.

G: Let me do it for you.

A: You are really very helpful and thoughtful. We are very lucky to have you as our tour guide. You have left me a very good impression, and I am deeply moved by your hospitality and your professional moral.

G: Oh, thank you. It's a great honor for me as your tour guide. I'd like to thank you all for the support and cooperation you have given to me. Wait for me please. (After a while), Here is the receipt of the airport fee.

B: Thanks again. Here is my name card, please feel free to get in touch with me.

G: Sure, I will. I'm looking forward to meeting you in the future. I think it's time for you to check in. Let me help you with the formalities. You need to weigh your bags in the baggage area. And then fill the immigration information cards in the immigration area. If you run into any difficulty, I'll be here to assist you immediately.

A: Fine. Can I carry this knife with me?

G: I'm afraid not. Please keep your invoice of the knife well, you need to show it when you go through the Customs.

A: Ok. Thank you very much. Bye-bye.

G: I wish you a good trip! Bye-bye.

1. When will be the appropriate time to bid farewell to the tourists?

2. How should a tour guide respond to tourist's requests to go shopping by themselves?

3. When will be the appropriate time to arrive at the airport?

4. If a British tourist intends to purchase ancient Chinese porcelain, what should a guide advise him?

5. What should be done to avoid missing a plane?

6. What should a guide do when a tourist finds his luggage missed upon arrival at the local airport?

7. Who should pay for the departure tax at the airport?

8. What have you learned from this dialogue?

9. What should you check before leaving for airport?

10. Write a farewell speech within 200 words?

5 **Try to fill in the following chart about the basic elements of a farewell speech.**

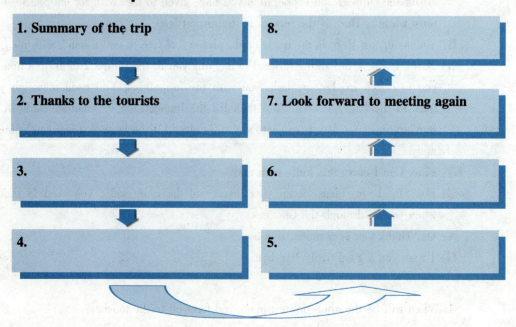

1. Summary of the trip
2. Thanks to the tourists
3.
4.
5.
6.
7. Look forward to meeting again
8.

6 Rewrite the following speech into a dialogue and practice with your partners.

A Farewell Speech

Distinguished guests, ladies and gentlemen,

Good morning. Time goes so quickly, your trip to China is drawing to a close. Ten days ago, we met as strangers. Today, we bid farewell to each other as friends. Your duration of stay in this country was only two weeks. We have visited Beijing, which is the capital of the People's Republic of China, then we visited Guilin and Hangzhou, I hope you'll take back happy memories of your trip to China. Yet it's time to say goodbye, as every good thing must have an ending. I will take this last opportunity to say something by way of a farewell.

Firstly, I'd like to express my thanks to our tour leader, Mr. White, for his help and cooperation. I am profoundly grateful to all of your for the cooperation and support you have given to me during your trip. You have been very attentive during my introduction. And you have been kind enough to offer me suggestions on guiding skills, English learning and culture differences. As we all know, language and culture are indispensable. The best way for an English language learner is practice. Traveling with you enable me to improve my oral English. I would like to tell you that it had been a great pleasure for me to spend these days as your tour guide. I'd like to add that you are the best group we've ever been with. I would also like to deliver my appreciation to our driver, without your support, our visit would have been impossible.

As you have probably observed, China is developing very quickly. When and if you come back in the future, the country may have changed greatly. In order to make your future visit more enjoyable, I sincerely hope that you can leave your valuable suggestions with us. I do apologize for any unhappiness caused by my mistake during the trip. I'll miss all of you and hope to see you again in the future and to be your guide again. I hope you will enjoy your flight to London.

Once again, thank you for your cooperation and support. Bon voyage!

VOCABULARY ASSISTANT

bid 祝愿
farewell 告别,辞别
duration 为期
Bon voyage [法]再见,一路顺风(平安)

7 **Cultural Salon: Read the following passage, try to get some cultural knowledge about *Chinese arts and crafts* and answer the questions.**

It is common knowledge that China has a long history in both art and tradition crafts. Painted pottery appeared in China 6,000 years ago. The most representative of all the Chinese arts and crafts are bronze wares, jade carvings and lacquer wares of the Shang and Zhou dynasties, silk fabrics of the Han and Tang dynasties, embroidery of the Song Dynasty, porcelain and cloisonné of the Ming and Qing dynasties. Besides, China's basketry, calligraphy, music, opera, painting, paper-cut, seals, bonsai, silk flowers, kites and toys are also well known with their strong artistry and national flavor. They are not only a vivid reflection of Chinese culture but also the wisdom and perfect craftsmanship of Chinese people.

We are all clear that in China there are countless types of arts and crafts. Therefore we can only have a light touch on some of them.

Bronze vessels invented some 5,000 years ago that led our ancestors into the bronze era. Bronze can be classified into four main types based on function: food vessels, wine vessels, water vessels and musical instruments. Within each group are endless variations ranging in design and form, fully demonstrating the rich imagination and creativity of the ancient Chinese people.

Jade has a history in China of at least five thousands years. The jade comes in two forms, nephrite and jadeite. Jadeite can be easily broken for it only forms under great pressure and heat. But nephrite is the world's toughest stone which is even stronger than diamond. Jade is found contained within the development of religion and civilization, having moved from the use of decoration on to the rites of worship and burial. It is believed to possess magical powers and is associated with merit, morality, grace and dignity. No other culture has valued jade for such high spiritual position.

Carved lacquer ware is one of the traditional Chinese arts and crafts. It can be dated back as early as the New Stone Age. Traditional Chinese lacquer art applies natural lacquer liquid from lacquer trees. The core material can be everything, ranging from wood or bamboo to metal or even plastic. Then coated with red or black lacquer on its surface, and then engraving designs on the lacquer. Chinese lacquer art came into its golden age during the Han Dynasty. From the Shang Dynasty to the Han, colorful painting, gold inlaying and other techniques were introduced into the making of lacquer ware.

1. What are the best representatives of all the Chinese arts and crafts in your opinion?

2. Do you know any other Chinese traditional arts and crafts apart from above mentioned?

3. Does jade in China contain any special meaning?

4. Which kind of Chinese art or craft interest you most? Why?

5. Can you provide a creative plan to develop Chinese traditional arts and crafts?

Further reading: Chinese Arts and Crafts

Ladies and gentlemen,

Good morning, today I will give you a further introduction to Chinese arts and crafts for you on the way to National Arts and Crafts Museum. The museum located on the fifth floor of Guomei Department Store. It is a national level art museum focused on displaying, collecting the modern artists works in China. It is the first professional arts and crafts in Beijing.

The four sections of this art museum house arts and crafts, national folk art, Beijing folk art and modern folk art. Magnificent jade ware, richly decorated lacquer, elegantly molded and painted earthenware and most delicate embroidery are all on exhibition here. They were carefully selected from all over the country by a panel of art historians and artists. I must say that the exhibition we will visit is not only a rare feast for our eyes but also a shock for our heart. Now I'll introduce some Chinese arts and crafts to you.

Chinese porcelain is worldwide known for its beautiful white color, its clear bell-like sound and its thin walls. A proverb goes like that "whiter than jade and thinner than paper". It has been one of the earliest artworks introduced to the western world through the Silk Road. The first porcelain in China was made during the Shang Dynasty. One of the first production places for porcelain ware was Gaoling in Shanxi, a town that gave its name to one raw material for chinaware, kaolin. They were made in the form of all kinds of items for daily use due to its durability. Porcelain began to develop and the artworks were introduced westward in the Han Dynasty; most daily used porcelain were replaced by gold, silver, jade and other materials during the Tang Dynasty. Jade became a fashion again in the Song Dynasty. The blue and white porcelain was invented after well developed in the Yuan Dynasty. Jade is still a brilliant art through the development of 4,000 years.

We have enjoyed ancient Chinese ceramic and pottery in the Palace Museum. The National Art Museum of China will show us modern and contemporary Chinese ceramic and pottery art. The museum offers audio and touch-screen guides and videos about the history of Chinese porcelain and the featured artists for visitors. And you can also follow the lecturers in each hall.

Ladies and gentlemen, here we are. I'll give you one and half hours to visit the museum. We will meet right here. Hope you enjoy your visit!

8 Work in Pairs.

Student A You are a European tourist to China.

Student B You are a tour guide.

Student A asks Student B to introduce some Chinese arts and crafts.

9 Supplementary task: Introduce one of Chinese arts and crafts you are interested in. Make a presentation within ten minutes in class. The teacher and students will make comments on if you address the main points about Chinese arts and crafts, and tell you how the presentation can be improved.

Peer's Assessment Form

	A	B	C	D
1. Delivery				
1.1 Is the articulation or intonation unnatural?	☐	☐	☐	☐
1.2 Is the presentation skillful and practical?	☐	☐	☐	☐
1.3 Are there any unclear expressions or unfinished sentences?	☐	☐	☐	☐
1.4 Is the voice unpleasant or unconvincing?	☐	☐	☐	☐
1.5 Are the main points outstanding?	☐	☐	☐	☐
2. Language				
2.1 Are there any irritating mispronunciations?	☐	☐	☐	☐
2.2 Are there any irritating grammatical mistakes?	☐	☐	☐	☐
2.3 Are there any unidiomatic expressions?	☐	☐	☐	☐
3. Coherence				
3.1 Are there any abrupt beginnings or endings?	☐	☐	☐	☐
3.2 Is the performance incoherent?	☐	☐	☐	☐
3.3 Is the message implausible or illogical?	☐	☐	☐	☐
4. Expressions and Appearance				
4.1 Are the expression and appearance natural?	☐	☐	☐	☐
5. Attitude and ability				
5.1 Is the attitude active and conscientious?	☐	☐	☐	☐
5.2 Is the presentation very effective?	☐	☐	☐	☐

Final Comments

Student's Feedback

Teacher's Comments

The candidate has met the standard, knowledge and skill requirements.

Candidates: _____   Date _____

Assessor: _____   Date _____

Vocabulary

A

abhidharma *n.* 论藏	Unit 8
abundance *n.* 丰富	Unit 7
accommodation *n.* 住处,膳宿	Unit 4
acrobatic show 杂技表演	Unit 2
acrobatics *n.* 杂技	Unit 10
agreeable *adj.* 宜人的	Unit 9
alchemy *n.* 炼金术	Unit 8
Altair *n.* [天]牵牛星	Unit 4
altar *n.* 祭坛	Unit 9
ambience *n.* 气氛	Unit 8
ambiguity *n.* 含糊,不明确	Unit 4
Amitabha Buddha 阿弥陀佛	Unit 8
anthology *n.* 诗选,文选	Unit 4
antique *n.* 古物,古董	Unit 10
archaeological *adj.* 考古学的	Unit 4&7
archery *n.* 射箭	Unit 9
Arhat *n.* 阿罗汉	Unit 8
aroma *n.* 芳香	Unit 6
array *vi.* 部署	Unit 7
arrival & departure time 抵离时间	Unit 1
ascetic *n.* 苦行者	Unit 8
assiduous *adj.* 勤勉的	Unit 7
astronomy *n.* 天文学	Unit 1
Athens *n.* 雅典(希腊首都)	Unit 4
attentive *adj.* 注意的,专心的	Unit 10
authentic *adj.* 正宗的	Unit 9&10
Avatamsaka Sutra 华严经	Unit 8
awestruck *adj.* 敬畏的	Unit 5

B

banquet *n.* 宴会	Unit 10
banyan *n.* 菩提树,印度榕树	Unit 4
basketry *n.* 篓编织品,编制工艺	Unit 10
benevolence *n.* 仁	Unit 5
bid *v.* 祝愿	Unit 10
blockhouse *n.* 碉堡	Unit 7
bodhi tree 菩提树	Unit 8
Bodhisattva *n.* 菩萨	Unit 8
bonsai *n.* 盆景	Unit 10
bristle *vi.* 竖起	Unit 7
brochure *n.* 宣传册	Unit 3
Buddha of Immeasurable Life 无量寿佛	Unit 8
bund *n.* 码头	Unit 4

C

Cairo *n.* 开罗(埃及首都)	Unit 4
calligrapher *n.* 书法家	Unit 6
calligraphy *n.* 书法	Unit 7
causeway *n.* 铺道	Unit 6
cavalry *v.* 骑兵	Unit 7
ceramic *n.* 陶瓷制品	Unit 10
chariot *n.* 战车	Unit 7
charter *v.* 租,包(船、车等)	Unit 4
chisel *v.* 砍凿	Unit 7
chromium *n.* 铬	Unit 7
chrysanthemum *n.* 菊花	Unit 7
civilization *n.* 文明	Unit 7
cloisonné *n.* 景泰蓝瓷器	Unit 10
coincide *vi.* 一致,符合	Unit 10
complex *n.* 综合建筑	Unit 5
concentration *n.* 禅定静虑	Unit 8
confirm *v.* 确认	Unit 1
conspicuous *adj.* 显著的	Unit 7

contact v. 联系	Unit 1	exquisitely adv. 精巧地	Unit 7
continental adj. 大陆性的	Unit 5	extra adj. 额外的	Unit 3
conventions n. 风俗	Unit 8		
cowherd n. 牧牛者	Unit 4	**F**	
crescent n. 月牙	Unit 6	fascinating adj. 很有吸引力	Unit 5
cube n. 立方体	Unit 3	fermented adj. 发酵的	Unit 9
customary adj. 习惯的, 惯例的	Unit 10	ferocious adj. 凶猛的	Unit 9
cypress n. 柏树	Unit 7	fertile v. 富饶的	Unit 7
		fidelity n. 忠诚	Unit 5
D		flexibility n. 适应性, 机动性	Unit 7
decrepitude n. 衰老	Unit 8	flock n. 一群(羊)	Unit 9
delicacy n. 美味佳肴	Unit 4	flute n. 长笛	Unit 4
deliver v. 运;送	Unit 3	flying apsaras 飞天	Unit 7
depart v. 出发	Unit 1	formality n. 手续	Unit 3
departure n. 离开	Unit 3	fresco n. 壁画	Unit 8
destination n. (旅游)目的地	Unit 1&3&4		
devastating adj. 令人震惊的	Unit 5	**G**	
dharma n. 达摩	Unit 8	Gelugpa Order 格鲁派	Unit 8
dignified adj. 有威严的	Unit 5	gender n. 性别	Unit 1
disembark v. (使)起岸, (使)登陆	Unit 10	genre n. 类型, 流派	Unit 4
distinctively adv. 区别地	Unit 2	gigantic adj. 巨大的	Unit 5
distribute v. 分配, 分给	Unit 3	gingko n. 银杏	Unit 6
distribution n. 分布	Unit 6&10	grain n. 粒状物	Unit 3
dominant adj. 占主要地位的	Unit 9	greasy adj. 油腻的	Unit 3
Douniu n. 斗牛	Unit 5	Greenwich Mean Time 格林尼治标准时间	Unit 2
dragon n. 龙	Unit 5	grotto n. 洞穴	Unit 7&9
durability n. 经久, 耐久力	Unit 10	gulp v. 吞咽;饮	Unit 9
dynasticism n. 王朝统治	Unit 6		
		H	
E		Hangshi n. 行什	Unit 5
elixir n. 炼金药, 不生不老	Unit 8	harmony n. 协调	Unit 5
embroidery n. 刺绣品, 刺绣	Unit 10	have a headcount 清点人数	Unit 1
emotional adj. 情感的	Unit 2	Heavenly Steed n. 天马	Unit 5
emphasize v. 强调	Unit 3	herd n. 牧人	Unit 9
encyclopedia n. 百科全书	Unit 6	hilarity n. 热闹	Unit 2
entrance tickets 门票	Unit 1	Hinayana Buddhism 小乘佛教	Unit 8
erode v. 侵蚀;腐蚀	Unit 9	hold a sign 手举接站牌	Unit 1
ethnic adj. 民族的	Unit 9	Homo sapiens 智人	Unit 5
etiquette n. 礼节	Unit 5		
evolution v. 进展, 演变, 进化	Unit 7	**I**	
excavate v. 挖掘	Unit 7	immense adj. 极广大的	Unit 5
excavation n. 出土文物	Unit 4	immortality n. 长生	Unit 8
excursion n. 游览, 参观	Unit 9&10	imperial adj. 皇帝的	Unit 6
exhausted adj. 耗尽的, 疲惫的	Unit 4	incense n. 香	Unit 9
exotic adj. 异国情调的	Unit 9	incorporated adj. 合成一体的	Unit 5

indispensable adj. 不可缺少的,绝对必要的　Unit 2&10
inferior adj. 下等的,次的　Unit 5
inhabitant n. 居民,居住者　Unit 4
inlay n. 镶嵌　Unit 10
inscription n. 碑铭　Unit 7
intelligence n. 智力　Unit 5
interact vi. 互相作用　Unit 10
invoice n. 发票,发货单　Unit 10
itinerary n. 旅行计划;旅游线路　Unit 1&4

J

jadeite n. [矿物]硬玉　Unit 4&10
jataka n. 本生经　Unit 8

L

labyrinth n. 迷宫　Unit 9
lacquer n. 漆,漆器　Unit 4&10
laid-back adj. 松弛的;自在的　Unit 9
lido n. 海滨浴场　Unit 9
limestone n. 石灰石　Unit 9
local guide 地陪　Unit 2
lunar calendar 阴历　Unit 1

M

Madrid n. 马德里(西班牙首都)　Unit 5
Mahayana Buddhism 大乘佛教　Unit 8
majestic adj. 宏伟的,庄严的　Unit 4
mandarin duck 鸳鸯　Unit 6
Manjusri n. 文殊菩萨　Unit 8
marsh n. 湿地,沼泽地　Unit 4
marshland n. 沼泽地　Unit 7
mausoleum n. 王的陵墓　Unit 7
Medicine Buddha 药师佛　Unit 8
mendicant n. 乞丐　Unit 8
meridian adj. 子午的　Unit 5
merit n. 优点,价值　Unit 10
metallurgical adj. 冶金学的　Unit 7
metalwork n. 金属制品　Unit 2
military adj. 军事的　Unit 7
miniascape n. 盆景　Unit 6
miscellaneous adj. 混杂的　Unit 4
monument n. 纪念碑　Unit 5
mural n. 壁画　Unit 7
mutton n. 羊肉　Unit 9
mythological adj. 神话的,虚构的　Unit 4

N

national guide 全陪　Unit 2
neolithic adj. 新石器时代的　Unit 4
nephrite n. [矿物]软玉　Unit 10
nirvana n. 涅槃　Unit 8
Nyingmapa Order 宁玛派　Unit 8

O

obscure adj. 使暗的　Unit 7
option n. 选项,选择权　Unit 4
orchestral n. 管弦乐的　Unit 5
outlaw n. 歹徒,逃犯　Unit 4
overshadow v. 遮蔽,使……失色　Unit 10

P

Padmasambhava n. 莲花生大士　Unit 8
Panchen Lama 班禅喇嘛　Unit 6
panoramic adj. 全景的　Unit 5
passion n. 热情　Unit 9
pebble n. 鹅卵石　Unit 9&4
peephole n. 窥视孔　Unit 7
peninsula n. 半岛　Unit 9
perch v. 位于　Unit 7
percussion n. 打击乐器　Unit 5
perspective n. 前景　Unit 7
phenomenal adj. 非凡的,显著的　Unit 5
Philadelphia n. 费城　Unit 5
phoenix n. 凤　Unit 5
picturesque adj. 景色如画的　Unit 9
pilgrimage n. 朝圣　Unit 4&8
porcelain n. 瓷器,瓷　Unit 10
porter n. 行李员　Unit 1
Potala Palace 布达拉宫　Unit 8
preserve v. 保存　Unit 5
Princess Tritsun 尺尊公主(尼泊尔)　Unit 8
Princess Wencheng 文成公主　Unit 8
principal adj. 主要的　Unit 7
prolong v. 延长,拖延　Unit 10
pungent adj. 刺鼻;辛辣的　Unit 3
puppet n. 傀儡　Unit 4
purity n. 纯净　Unit 5

Q

quadrangle n. 四边形,方院　Unit 5

R

realm *n.* 界	Unit 8
recognizable *adj.* 可辨认的	Unit 2
Red Palace 红宫	Unit 8
reed *n.* 芦苇,芦笛	Unit 4
regulation *n.* 规律	Unit 9
reincarnation *n.* 化身	Unit 8
restrict *n.* 限制	Unit 7
reverent *adj.* 虔诚的	Unit 8
rhythmical *adj.* 节奏的	Unit 5
rickshaw *n.* 黄包车,人力车	Unit 10
righteousness *n.* 义	Unit 5
rites *n.* 礼	Unit 5
rodeo *n.* 马术比赛	Unit 9
run its course 按常规发展	Unit 7

S

sacred *adj.* 神的,神圣的	Unit 4
sacrifices *n.* 祭品	Unit 1
sauté *v.* 炒;嫩煎	Unit 3
scatter *n.* 散落,分散	Unit 9
scheduled *adj.* 预定的	Unit 4
scripture *n.* 经文	Unit 8&9
sculpture *n.&v.* 雕刻	Unit 4&6
secular *n.* 世俗	Unit 8
segment *n.* 段	Unit 3
semi-humid *adj.* 半湿热	Unit 5
sentient beings 众生	Unit 8
severely *adv.* 严格地	Unit 7
Shakyamuni Buddha 释迦牟尼佛	Unit 8
shred *n.* 细条	Unit 3
shrine *n.* 圣地,神祠	Unit 9
sightseeing *n.* 观光	Unit 10
signify *n.* 表示	Unit 2
silt *n.* 淤沙	Unit 9
simmer *v.* 炖	Unit 3
site of enlightenment 道场	Unit 8
solar term 节气	Unit 1
Songtsen Gampo 松赞干布	Unit 8
souvenir *n.* 纪念品	Unit 10
splendid *adj.* 壮丽的,极好的	Unit 10
squid *n.* 鱿鱼	Unit 3
stalactite *n.* 钟乳石	Unit 9
stalagmite *n.* 石笋	Unit 9
strategically *adv.* 战略上	Unit 7
stretch *v.* 伸展	Unit 7
Suanni *n.* 狻猊	Unit 5
subdivided *adj.* 细分的	Unit 5
sublime *n.* 庄严	Unit 6
supreme *adj.* 至高的	Unit 5
surcharge *n.* 额外收费	Unit 3
symposium *n.* 讨论会	Unit 2

T

Tanjur *n.*《丹珠尔》(藏传佛教大藏经之《论藏》)	Unit 8
Taoist philosophy 道教哲学	Unit 7
terracotta *n.* 陶瓦,赤土陶器	Unit 4
the Dragon Boat Festival 端午节	Unit 1
the Forbidden City 故宫	Unit 2
the Lantern Festival 元宵节	Unit 1
the Mid-Autumn Festival 中秋节	Unit 1
the Neolithic Period 新石器时代	Unit 7
the reception program 接待计划	Unit 1
the Spring Festival 春节	Unit 1
the Summer Palace 颐和园	Unit 2
the Temple of Heaven 天坛	Unit 2
thrust *v.* 插入	Unit 9
tongue-numbing *adj.* 舌头麻木的	Unit 3
tour guide certificate 导游证	Unit 1
tour leader 领队	Unit 1
tranquility *n.* 宁静	Unit 5
transportation *n.* 运输	Unit 7
tridimensional *adj.* 立体的	Unit 6
Tripitaka *n.* 三藏(经律论)	Unit 8
tropical *adj.* 热带的	Unit 9
Tsong Khapa 宗喀巴	Unit 8

U

union *n.* 联合	Unit 5
unparallel *adj.* 不平行的	Unit 9

V

valentine *n.* 情人,情人节礼物	Unit 4
Vega *n.* [天]织女星,织女	Unit 4
verbal *adj.* 口头的	Unit 4
vibrant *adj.* 动荡的	Unit 5
voucher *n.* 票据	Unit 1

W

White Palace 白宫   Unit 8
wicker *n.* 柳条   Unit 9
witchcraft *n.* 巫术   Unit 8
wrestle *n.* 摔跤   Unit 9

X

Xiezhi *n.* 獬豸   Unit 5

Y

Yayu *n.* 押鱼   Unit 5
yurt *n.* 蒙古包   Unit 9

Z

zeal *n.* 热心,热情   Unit 4

Answer Key

Unit 1

Start-up

Tourists 游客 Restaurants 餐厅 Arrival & departure time 抵离时间
Itinerary 旅游计划 Transportation 交通方式

1
1. Li Yang is a tour guide in China International Travel Service (CITS).
2. The tour group is from the United States.
3. She stands at a visible place of the exit, holding a sign highly.
4. I'm Li Yang, the local guide from China International Travel Service, Beijing branch.
5. Confirm the expected arriving time before departing.
   Contact the bus driver and travel with the bus to the airport.
   Arrive at the airport or the railway station 30 minutes ahead of expected arriving time.
   Confirm the parking place.
   Reconfirm the exact arriving time at the airport or the railway station.
   Contact the porter and inform him of the destination of luggage.
   Stand at a highly visible place of the exit holding a sign.

2
1. International 2. visible 3. branch 4. emergency 5. arrangements
6. check 7. departs from 8. headcount 9. entrance 10. corner

4
1. Confirm the expected arriving time before departing.
   Contact the bus driver and travel with the bus to the airport.
   Arrive at the airport or the railway station 30 minutes ahead of expected arriving time.
   Confirm the parking place.
   Reconfirm the exact arriving time at the airport or the railway station.
   Contact the porter and inform him of the destination of luggage.
   Stand at a highly visible place of the exit holding a sign.
2. Meet the tour group and contact the tour leader.
   Check the name, code of the tour group and the number of tourists.
   Check if all luggage has been claimed and collected by porter for transfer to the bus.
   Show the tour group to the bus and board the bus.
3. Receiving the tourists is the first step in your guiding job.

4. You should make sure of all the detailed information to the reception program.

5. Including the information of the tour group, tourists, arrival & departure time, itinerary, hotels, restaurants, transportation, vouchers, items for the guide and the tour group, etc.

6. Including name and code of this group, contacting person and telephone number of the organizing travel agency, number of the tourists, names of the tour leader and the national guide, language, etc.

7. Including arriving and departing times, transportation, hotels and rooms, restaurants and meals, scenic spots, meetings, banquets, etc.

8. Including number and price of the entrance tickets.

9. Check the name, code of the tour group and the number of tourists.
   Check if all the luggage have been claimed and collected by porter for transfer to the bus.

10. Lead the tour group to the bus outside the entrance and help the tourists to board the bus.

5 3. Arrive at the airport 30 minutes prior to the expected arriving time.

4. Reconfirm the exact arriving time at the airport.

5. Stand at a highly visible place of the exit holding a sign.

6. Meet the tour group and contact the tour leader to check the name, code of the tour group and the number of tourists.

7. Check if all luggage has been claimed and collected by porter for transfer to the bus.

8. Show the tour group to the bus and board the bus.

7 1. They are based on the Chinese lunar calendar.

2. Chinese families come together for a celebration dinner.

3. People watch lanterns.

4. Because people want to commemorate Qu Yuan, one of ancient China's famous poets.

5. Emperors followed the rite of offering sacrifices to the moon on the Mid-Autumn Festival in ancient China.

Unit 2

Start-up

Introduce (yourself, other colleagues, bus driver and the travel agency) 介绍(自己、同事、司机和旅行社)

Local weather 当地天气　　　　Itinerary and points for attention 旅游行程及注意事项

Bus number and cell phone number 车牌号及手机号码

1 1. China International Travel Service, Beijing Branch.

2. JH-05123.

3. Eight.

4. Five. They are the Forbidden City, the Summer Palace, the Temple of Heaven and the Great Wall.

5. Peking Opera, Acrobatic Show.

2 1. relax   2. colleague   3. rewarding   4. hesitate   5. luxurious
    6. reset   7. adopt   8. brilliant   9. itinerary   10. furthermore

4 1. Beijing Hotel is located at the entrance of Wangfujing Avenue, just 200 meters east of Tiananmen Square.
    2. 13 hours.
    3. It's a fine day and the highest temperature is 23 degree centigrade.
    4. Three. They are Yuan, Ming and Qing dynasties.
    5. Autumn and May.
    6. Thirty-four emperors.
    7. The 29th Olympic Games.
    8. Tiananmen Square, the Great Wall, the Forbidden City, the Temple of Heaven, the Summer Palace, and the ruins of Peking Man at Zhoukoudian.
    9. Over 13.8 million.
    10. Peking Roast Duck.

5 3. Provide the bus number and your mobile phone number.
    4. Give a brief introduction of the country and the city.
    5. Describe the itinerary briefly.
    6. Introduce the hotel briefly.
    7. Comment on the enroute scenery.
    8. Organize entertainment activities.

7 1. Chinese names are given in the reverse of Western names.
    2. Chinese people often greet friends or acquaintances by asking whether they have eaten or by asking where they are going.
    3. For breakfast, Chinese people generally eat congee (over-boiled rice), dumplings, or noodles.
    4. Green tea, black tea, brick tea, scented tea, and Oolong tea.
    5. It is a symbol of togetherness. It signifies respect and the sharing of something enjoyable with visitors.

Unit 3

Start-up

single room 单人间   double room 大床间   twin room 双床间
suite 套房   deluxe suite 豪华套房   studio room 小型公寓式套间
duplex 二层公寓式套间

1 1. Individual guests means that guests are no more than ten, there are no tour leader in the group; while group guests means that the number of the group is more than ten, as usual, there must be a tour leader in the group to take care of the guests.

2. While showing the individual guests to the hotel, the tour guide must remind them to get their passports ready, and he must tell some specific information of the guests to the front desk, such as the number of the guests, the number of the rooms, the name of the travel agency, the name of the person who reserves the rooms... etc., the hotel will ask the guests to fill in the form by themselves, at this time, the tour guide should help the guests who have difficulties.

3. The following information must be included although different hotels have different forms, they are: surname (family name), given name (first name), sex, age, date of birth, place of birth, nationality, passport number, reason of stay, arrival date, departure date, type of visa and signature.

4. The tour guide must tell them the location of the elevator, the time to get together, the place to get together and other necessary information.

5. The tour leader will have a group visa, and the necessary information of the guests is shown on it, so it's unnecessary for the guests to show their passports at the hotel.

2
1. individual guests
2. best service
3. reservation
4. formalities
5. registration form
6. room types
7. bother
8. group guests
9. tour leader
10. distribute

4
1. He must remind the guests of the time when they should get up, when the luggage should be out of rooms and when they should return their room keys, of course the departure time shouldn't be forgotten.
2. Yes, it is. He does so in order to avoid of being late for other activities.
3. The bellman of the hotel.
4. As usual, in early morning, the front desk must be very busy, because here is a regulation in all the hotels all over China.
5. Before 12:00 at noon.
6. Packing up their luggage.
7. I'm sorry to hear that. Don't worry, however, I'll help you.
8. Checking carefully and correct it.
9. The tourist who consumed should pay.
10. The tour guide.

5
1. Greeting
4. Asking the Guest to Fill in the Registration
6. Assigning Room-key Cards
8. Extending Best Wishes

7
1. Four Cuisines: Sichuan Cuisine, Shandong Cuisine, Guangdong Cuisine (Cantonese) and Zhejiang-Jiangsu Cuisine.

2. Sichuan cuisine is hot and tongue-numbing, Shandong cuisine is fresh, tasty but now greasy, Guangdong cuisine, also known as Cantonese in the world, is fresh, tender and light-seasoned, Jiangsu-Zhejiang cuisine is sweet and sour, the cutting technique and the temperature control are emphasized.
3. Sichuan cuisine: twice-cooked pork slices, spicy diced chicken with peanuts, dry-fried shark fin, fish-flavored pork shreds and pork-marked woman's bean curd.

   Shandong cuisine: yellow river carp in sweet and sour sauce, stewed/agate sea cucumber, Dezhou braised chicken, Beijing roast duck, shrimps wearing jade belts, eight immortals crossing the sea.

   Guangdong cuisine: dragon and tiger locked in battle, roast snake with chrysanthemum blooms, roast suckling pig, duck web in oyster sauce, braised chicken feet with wild herbs.

   Jiangsu-Zhejiang cuisine: crystal pork, braised shark fin in brown sauce, simmered pork head, eel and crab meat in crab shells, west lake fish in vinegar sauce.
4. They are chicken, duck, fish, pork, seafood, game, eggs, vegetables, soybean products, dairy products, fruits and nuts.
5. Quick-frying, stir-frying, roasting, sautéing, simmering, braising, smoking, steaming and stewing.

Unit 4

Start-up

Accommodation 膳宿	Transportation 交通	Entrance ticket 门票
Guide service 导游服务	Destination 目的地	Quoted price 报价
Scenery 风景,景色		

2
1. detailed
2. pleasant
3. preserved
4. rest
5. is eager to
6. according to
7. afraid
8. served
9. take
10. majestic

4
1. An itinerary is a detailed schedule for a journey.
2. The guide should double check the itinerary before receiving the tour group and verifies the itinerary with the national tour guide, tour leader, or independent tourists after the greeting.
3. Changes of times, dates, activities, lodging and meals during the tour.
4. After the visit is finished, some tourists require to prolong the visit, if the visa is valid, it's ok but better not. If the visa is inefficacy, the tour guide should refuse the request. If some tourist has to stay for special purpose, the tour guide should report it to the manager and then give him some necessary help according to the instructions of the manager. If the tourist is injured or sick and has to stay for a longer time in the

hospital, the tour guide should help him go through the procedure in the hospital. If some tourists require the travel agency for more service after the tour, he has to sign another contract with the travel agency.

5. I can not change a scheduled tour itinerary, but I can find a suitable time for tourists to go shopping.

　　When the tourists ask to change the route, the tour guide should follow the contract in principle. The tour guide shouldn't make any decision even if under particular conditions. He or she should report it to the travel agency and change the itinerary according to the instructions by the approval of the travel agency.

6. The tour itinerary is an introduction to the products of a travel agency, it help the travel agency to sell its products. After the payment, the tour itinerary will play an important role in controlling the quality of the whole journey.
7. We will visit an additional program after the scheduled program if time is possible.
9. The guide must gain approval of both the company and the guests and obtain signature of the tour leader or an independent traveler as well.
10. Omit.

5 3. Entrance fees　　4. Hotel accommodation　　5. Transportation
　　6. Tour guide　　　　7. Travel Insurance　　　　8. Quotation

7 1. There are different styles such as historical records, critical works, idioms, Poems, essays, allegories, ballads, Drama, novel and many legends in Chinese Classical Literature. The four masterpieces of Chinese classical literature is belong to the style of novel.
2. The four masterpieces of Chinese classical literature appeared during Ming and Qing dynasty.
3. They are famous for an extensive vista and scope, vivid and realistic characterization and elegant and evocative language.
4. Omit.
5. Omit.

Unit 5

Start-up

Latitude 纬度　　　　　　　　　　Location 位置
Ancient 古代的　　　　　　　　　 Modern 现代的
Panoramic view 全景

1 1. The suitable time to introduce a city is during your delivering a welcome speech or the time during a city tour. When you introduce a city, you'd better introduce the history, geography, scenery, economy, culture of the city.
2. Set up the image of the city, highlight the main characteristics, needn't attend to each and every aspect of a matter.

ANSEER KEY 135

3. Deliver a welcome speech, give a brief introduction of the city, introduce the hotel where tourists live and tell them your arrangement for tour.
4. Bird's Nest, Water Cube, the National Grand Theater, the Forbidden City, the Great Wall, Tiananmen Square, Chinese Revolution History Museum, Chairman Mao's Mausoleum, Great Hall of the People, the elegant and beautiful Tiananmen, the Ming Tombs, the Drum Tower built in the 1400's, Fragrant Hills Park and so on.
5. Records show that Beijing has been an inhabited city for more than three thousand years and has lived through invasions, devastating fires, dynasties, warlords, Anglo-French troops and has emerged each time as a strong and vibrant city. For more than 800 years, Beijing was a capital city from the Yuan Dynasty to the Ming and Qing dynasties. Thirty-four emperors have lived and ruled in Beijing and it has been an important trading city from earliest days.

2
1. located
2. semi-humid and continental
3. population
4. covers
5. Yuan Dynasty, Ming and Qing Dynasties
6. Thirty-four
7. economic, communications
8. ancestors

4
1. In early 15th century, the large-scale complex involved 100,000 artisans and one million workmen, took 14 years and was finished in 1420. The purpose is that the Palace Museum was the imperial palaces for emperors.
2. 24 emperors.
3. The Palace area is divided into two parts: the Outer Court and the Inner Palace. The former consists of the first three main halls, where the emperor received his courtiers and conducted grand ceremonies, while the latter was the living quarters for the imperial residence. At the rear of the Inner Palace is the Imperial Garden where the emperor and his family sought recreation.
4. Show that he is different from ordinary people and supreme position.
5. The river is spanned by five bridges, which were supposed to be symbols of the five virtues preached by Confucius—benevolence, righteousness, rites, intelligence, and fidelity.
6. The function of the Hall of Supreme Harmony is that the emperor held grand ceremonies here, such as the Winter Solstice, the Spring Festival, the emperor's birthday and enthronement, and the dispatch of generals to battles, etc.
7. The Outer Court consists mainly of the Hall of Supreme Harmony, the Hall of Complete Harmony, and the Hall of Preserving Harmony; the Inner Court is composed of the Palace of Heavenly Purity, the Hall of Union, and the Palace of Earthly Tranquility with three palaces on either side.
8. In the garden there are hundreds of pines, cypresses and various flowers, so the garden all year round fills the air with flowers' fragrance. In the northeastern corner of the gar-

den is a rock hill, known as the Hill of the Piled-up Wonders, on the top of which is a pavilion. At the foot of the hill are two fountains which jet two columns of water high into the air. It is said that on the ninth night of the ninth month of the lunar calendar, if a person climbs up a high place on that day, he would be safe from contagious diseases.

9. In the past, the imperial palace was in accessible to ordinary people and was walled up and heavily guarded. Only the emperor, empress, concubines, royal family members and eunuchs could live inside. Hence it was called the Forbidden City.

   The Forbidden City is also called the Purple Forbidden City. There are three arguments. One view holds that the word "purple" means an auspicious cloud, symbolized the emperor. Another argues that the word refers to the Purple Palace in heaven, where the Heavenly Emperor resides; the emperor on earth is the son of Heaven and should live in a palace compatible to the Purple Palace. A third view contents that the word "purple" is actually a reference to the Thuban galaxy and also symbolizes the emperor.

10. On the eave rafter of the Hall of Supreme Harmony there are 10 beasts named dragon, phoenix, lion, Heavenly Steed, Sea Horse, Suanni, Yayu, Xiezhi, Douniu and Hangshi. All these animals are given certain meanings. Dragon and phoenix symbolize the emperor and empress; the Heavenly Steed and Sea Horse stand for the imperial power; Douniu and Yayu are believe to be able to create clouds and rains to extinguish a fire. Lion is the king of beast. Suanni is an imaginary beast preying on tigers and leopards, therefore symbolizes leadership. Xiezhi is believed to have sharp eyes to distinguish between right and wrong and therefore stand for the open and aboveboard character of the emperor. The last animal looks like a monkey named Hangshi who is used for preventing from thunder, which ranks 10th of the 10 mascots.

5 Give a general idea of the Palace Museum, tell the location, size and area, introduce the architecture, layout, then according to the line of tour introduce the main halls one by one in order, at last give a comment on its historical value and position and so on.

3. Area
4. Architecture
5. Layout
6. Introduce for details
7. Comment

7 1. About 200 years ago.
2. Peking Opera combines literature with singing, dancing, musical dialogues, martial arts, colorful facial make-up and fantastic costumes. The music of Beijing opera is mainly orchestral music. The percussion instruments, in particular, provide a strongly rhythmical accompaniment to acting and make it extremely live and real.
3. In Peking Opera the roles are divided into four main types according to the sex, age, social status, and profession of the character. They are Sheng, Dan, Jing and Chou.
4. Omit.
5. Omit.

Unit 6

Start-up

Building reason 建造原因   Configuration 结构   Main parts 主要构成
Major sceneries 重要景点   Value 价值   Contribution 贡献

1
1. It is broad in scope, magnificent in construction, strong imperial symbolization.
2. From the geographic feature to the scenic spots distribution the garden is quite the same with the landform of China, so it can be looked as a miniature of our country.
3. Emperor Qianlong received Mongolian princes, Tibetan Panchen Lama and British envoy, McCartney in Ten-Thousand-Tree Garden.
4. In order to safeguard the unity of the multinational dynasticism and strengthen the northern frontier, in the 20th year of the reign of Kangxi, the Mulan Imperial Hunting Ground was built for the purpose of more political and military reasons than the onefold intention of hunting. It's about 150km north of Chengde city and 384km away from the Forbidden City in Beijing. It's necessary to set up some palaces along the way from Beijing to the Hunting Ground as the temporary resting places; one of them is today's Mountain Resort.
5. Liuhe in Buddhism means the harmonies of the heaven, earth, east, west, south and north.

2
1. imperial   2. miniature   3. fancy aroma   4. study
5. modeled after 6. sacrifice   7. crescent moon   8. valleys
9. royal gardens 10. freezing

4
1. It was set up by a high-rank official named Wang Xianchen. When lost court favor, he retired to Suzhou and turned to nature for sympathy. Wang thought that the life of planting trees, watering flowers, growing vegetables, meeting friends and doing suchlike things was a career of a humble administrator.
2. Three-fifth of its area taken up by water is the key feature of this garden.
3. Not too simple yet elegant, full of quiet vitality.
4. Omit.
5. It consists of three major parts: east, west and central.
6. The builder tried to make artificially a small world of their own, so all the points of an ideal living surroundings should be involved in one construction. They intended to create a landscape that could include as many beautiful types of scenery as possible in the limited space, the well-arranged rockeries, bridges, ponds and pavilions will give people the feeling that they live in a harmonious manmade nature.
7. The inverted vermeil railing of a stone bridge reflected in the water forms a rainbow-like scene, and the name comes from this wonderful view.

8. The center part.
9. There are no pillars inside the hall, the latticed glass windows are symmetrically fixed in all the four sides. Sitting in the hall one can indulge viewing the landscapes in all directions.
10. Omit.

5 3. Key feature of this garden
4. Three parts and relative scenic spots
5. Builder's intention to create the garden
6. Characteristics of private garden

7 1. Generally speaking, there are six major categories. They are green tea, black tea, scented tea, oolong tea, white tea and pressed tea.
2. Green tea is not fermented, the leaves and soup are green and it has natural fragrant smell. Black tea is fully fermented with "red" leaves and "red" soup. Scented tea, which smells of flowers, is made by mixing green tea with flower petals through elaborate working way. Oolong tea is semi-fermented; the leaf of this kind of tea is green in center with red edge around. Oolong tea possesses both the nature of black tea and green tea, mellowness and freshness. White tea is not fermented and leaves are not kneaded. The pressed tea is of special kind. Putting steamed green tea, black tea or scented tea into brick or ball shape tools and pressed then out of this type of tea.
3. Tea has medical and healthy functions. It's good to drink tea moderately, but if overdrinking side effects may happen.
4. Omit.
5. The pressed tea is a ball-shape or brick-shape tea, more convenient to take.

Unit 7

Start-up

Wonder 奇迹　　　　　Defensive 防御用的　　　　Dragon 龙
Beacon tower 烽火台　　Strategic 战略的

1 1. The Great Wall starts from Shanhaiguan Pass along the coast of the Bohai Sea in the east and ends in Jiayuguan Pass in Gansu Province in the west, traveling about 12,700 kilometers across Liaoning, Hebei, Beijing, Shanxi, Shanxi, Inner Mongolia, Ningxia and Gansu. So we call the Great Wall "Ten Thousand Li Wall". It winds its way westward over the vast territory of China from the bank of the Yalu River in Liaoning Province and ends at the foot of snowcapped Qilianshan and Tianshan mountains.
2. The Great Wall at Jinshanling.
3. Barrier walls, called "Zhangqiang", are a series of small walls on top of the Great Wall. They have peepholes and firing holes used to prevent the enemy from going ahead and approaching the blockhouses.

ANSEER KEY 139

4. The screen wall with the unicorn relievo on the top of the small Fox-head Tower is one of characteristics of the Great Wall. Barrier walls is another characteristic of construction rarely seen in other sections of the Great Wall. Bricks with Chinese characters are the third characteristic of the Great Wall and the unique section of the Great Wall.

5. In 1987.

2
1. bristle
2. territory
3. defensive
4. Heritage
5. shelter
6. approaching
7. complete
8. invaders
9. symbol
10. embody

4
1. Qin Shihuang, also called Ying Zheng, was the first emperor in Qin Dynasty.
2. The mausoleum is located at 5 kilometers east of Lintong, standing 76 meters high against the slopes of Mt. Lishan and facing thee Huishui River, which was built in 247 B.C. when Qin Shihuang ascended the throne at the age of 13.
3. The magnificent underground palace is divided into two parts called the inner and outer cities. The inner city is a square and the outer is a rectangle, 2,500 meters wide and 6,200 meters long. It took over 700,000 people 36 years to build it. In 1979, 1989 and 1994, three vaults were officially open to the public.
4. Omit.
5. In March 1974, peasants in Lintong County, 30 kilometers east of Xi'an, came across a piece of an earthen figure when digging a well, leading to the great discovery of terra-cotta warriors and horses which is a part of the Mausoleum of Qin Shihuang.
6. All of the clay warriors held real weapons in their hands and face east, showing Emperor Qin Shihuang's strong determination of wiping out the six states and unifying the whole country.
7. Omit.
8. What are the characteristics of the terra-cotta warriors?
   The figures vary from one another in expression, clothes, color, posture and hair-style. Some are standing, some are kneeling. The way to distinguish between officers and soldiers is whether they wear hats. The officers all wear hats, but soldiers don't. Senior officers wear colored scaled armor; intermediate-level officers wear colored, yellow-brimmed front or side armor; and low-ranking officers wear plain armors. Soldiers' armor is larger in size and fewer in number of plates than that of officers. The terra-cotta warriors display a unique personality from their expressions. The generals stand tall and strong, scintillating with wisdom and sophistication; officers look serious, staunch and clam; the soldiers are alert, brave and dauntless.
9. What kinds of the technology of manufacturing the bronze chariots and horses were used?
   According to a preliminary study, the technology of manufacturing the bronze chariots

and horses has involved casting, welding, revetting, inlaying embedding and chiseling. The excavation of the bronze chariots and horses provides extremely valuable material and data for the textual research of the metallurgical technique, the mechanism of the chariot and technological modeling of the Qin Dynasty.

10. Why do people say the Mausoleum is an important archaeological discovery in the world?
The Mausoleum is an important archaeological discovery in the world, which is a valuable file for further study of the politics, military affairs, economy, culture and art of the Qin Dynasty. Chinese art critics consider the excavation of the 2,000-year-old terra-cotta figures an unprecedented event in the history of both Chinese and world sculpture.

5 4. Introduce the mausoleum.
5. Characteristics
6. Value

7 1. Writing brush, ink stick, inkstone and paper are used.
2. Chinese calligraphy is original from the hieroglyphs, in the process of evolution, it gradually has formed various styles and schools and become an important part of the heritage of national culture.
3. The blue-and-green landscape used bright blue, green and red pigments derived from minerals to create a richly decorative style. The ink-and-wash landscape relied on vivid brushwork with varying degrees of intensity of ink to express the artist's conception of nature, his own emotions and individuality.
4. Bird and Flower painting was separated from decorative art in the 9th century. Many well-known artists painted in this genre during the Song Dynasty and their themes included a variety of flowers, fruits, insects and fish. Many of the scholarly painters working with ink and brush illustrate plum blossoms, orchids, bamboo, chrysanthemums, pines and cypresses, which reflect their own ideals and character.
5. Omit.

Unit 8

Start-up

Proportion 面积　　　　Configuration 结构　　　　Major parts 主要部分
Building reason 建造原因　Buddhism sect 佛教派别　　Tenet 教义

1 1. The following aspects should be involved: name, location, trait, background, historical events, configuration and so on. For example, Potala is Tibetan transliteration, namely Puto Luo, which means the place that bodhisattva lives. It is seated on the Mabu Mountain that locates in Lhasa city; it is not only a group of buildings involved the ancient architectural style of the palace, fort and temple together, but also the cultural treasure manifested the soul of the Tibetan Buddhism. Potala Palace includes four major parts. It was built to commemorate a historical fact etc.

ANSEER KEY 141

2. Four major parts: the Red Palace and the White Palace on the Red Mountain, the Dragon King Pond to the back of the mountain and the "snow" area at the foot of the mountain.

3. The Red Palace was built after the death of the Fifth Dalai Lama and for generations it serves as the Dalai tope palace and Buddha worshipping place, also the symbol of the Buddha world and the center of the space. The White Palace usually serves for secular affairs— the political headquarter and Dalai Lamas' residence.

4. They are the desire realm, the form realm and the formless realm.

5. The fifth and the thirteenth Dalai Lamas are regarded to be the greatest in history.

2
1. cultural heritage
2. murals
3. political headquarter
4. ascended
5. overall layout
6. three-realm
7. stupa, sandalwood
8. Red Palace, apex
9. survival
10. Dragon King Pond

4
1. Since the climate in the mountains is chilly, so it's also named the Cool Mountain.

2. Wutai Mountain is worldwide famous for its being looked up to as the Buddhist sacred land—one of the five main Buddhist holy lands in the world and ranks first among the four main Buddhist Mountains in China.

3. Manjusri is one of the Four Great Bodhisattvas, the one with the greatest wisdom, often placed on the left of Sakyamuni and always rides on a lion.

4. Wutai Mountain treasures many kinds of ancient architectures of China, from the Dynasty of the Tang, Song, Liao, Jin, Yuan, Ming, Qing to the Republic of China all left buildings of typical types.

5. The Beamless hall in the temple is a complete-brick building, so the complete brick structure is one of the distinguished features of Xiantong temple. Daxiong Precious Hall is complete wood-form frame. The world-known Bronze Hall was made of complete bronze by casting. So the complete bronze structure is another feature of Xiantong temple.

6. A statue of Buddha of Immeasurable Life is worshipped here, so also called Wuliang Hall.

7. Omit.

8. Among all the temples, Xian Tong Temple is the earliest, the oldest and the biggest

9. Another name of this hall is Large Buddha Hall, it is the main building in Xiantong temple, occupies about 600 sqm. The particular feature of the hall is its complete wood-form frame. In the hall three worlds Buddha statues are worshipped, Shakyamuni Buddha in the middle, Amitabha Buddha in the west and Medicine Buddha in the east, 18 Arhat statues sit on each side. The place is also used for holding grand Buddhist activities.

10. They are Shakyamuni Buddha in the middle, Amitabha Buddha in the west and Medicine Buddha in the east.

5
3. What is famous for
4. Characteristics of Xiantong temple
5. Some other sights
6. Manjusri belief

7 1. One day he went out to the street, the old, the sick, the poor and the corpses he saw revealed to him another aspect of life he never lived as a prince, which made him give up the life of a prince.

2. The four noble truths are: first, the truth of suffering; second, the truth of the arising of suffering; third, the truth of the cessation of suffering; fourth, the truth of the path to the cessation of suffering. The correct eightfold path are: (1) right view; (2) right thought; (3) right speech; (4) right action; (5) right livelihood; (6) right effort; (7) right mindfulness; (8) right concentration.

3. They are Mahayana Buddhism which is also called Great Vehicle or Bodhisattva Vehicle and Hinayana Buddhism which is also called Small Vehicle or Liberated Vehicle Buddhism.

4. Buddhism plays an important part in our life, especially Mahayana Buddhism .It brought to Chinese literature new conceptions, literary styles, and techniques of word-building in language. Buddhist painting and sculpture have left a rich source of material for the study of Chinese art and history, which highlight a brilliant chapter in China's cultural history. China's music, astronomy, medicine, and gymnastics all reflect the influences of the Mahayana Buddhism.

5. Hinayana Buddhism strives to become an Arhat, a person who has single-heartedly overcome his passions and ego, thereby gaining liberation for himself. It emphasis on individual self-liberation and claims Buddha as a historical figure, keeping the monastic life as virtue and the Tripitaka as authority.

Unit 9

Start-up
Green hills 翠绿的山峦
Fresh air 新鲜空气
Vast grasslands 宽阔的草原
Mushroom-like yurts 蘑菇一样的毡房
Unpolluted and quiet environment 未污染的幽静环境
Stunning cliffs 绝美的崖壁
Wild flowers 野花

1 1. It is situated in the northeast of Guangxi Zhuang Autonomous Region and on the west bank of the Lijiang River.

2. The average temperature of Guilin is about 18℃ with the lowest down to 8℃ in the coldest day of the winter and up to no more than 28℃ in the hottest day of the summer. That's the reason why you can visit Guilin all the year round and of course in Guilin, there is no low tourist season.

3. First., the Elephant Trunk Hill. It is shaped very much like a giant elephant standing by the riverside, gulping water from the river with its trunk dipping into it. It was formerly known as Li Hill and because one end of the hill looks like the elephant trunk, so comes the name of the Elephant Trunk and it is also a symbol of Guilin city.

Second, Seven kilometers northwest of the city center, the Reed Flute Cave(芦笛

洞) is the most magnificent cave in Guilin. It derives its name from the reeds at its entrance, which were once used to make flutes. It was in the Tang dynasty that local people discovered this cave. The huge karst cave is about 500 meters deep and 240 meters wide. In the cave, there are a lot of stalactites, stalagmites, stone screens, stone flowers and stone pillars of fantastic shapes. They seem to tell the visitors why the cave is known also as a place of natural art. Their shapes suggest images of old trees, dense shrubs, ferocious beasts and human figures. Especially the vast grotto, known as the crystal palace, is capable of holding some 1000 people.

Last, A visit to Guilin is not complete without a boat excursion down the Lijiang River to Yangshuo, about 83 km from Guilin city. The tourists must be attracted by the picturesque sceneries on both banks of the river. As everyone knows, "Guilin has the most beautiful scenery in China, and Yangshuo is the most beautiful part of Guilin."

4. About 300 million years ago, here used to be a vast ocean. The upheaval movement of the earth crust sent the limestone on the sea-bed up above the water, which exposed, weathered and eroded for long time in the air has become forests of peaks of fantastic shapes, labyrinths of dissolved caves and marvelous rivers under the ground.

5. Guilin has the most beautiful scenery in China, and Yangshuo is the most beautiful part of Guilin.

2
1. situated
2. subtropical
3. average
4. Karst
5. Elephant Trunk Hill
6. city center
7. Dragon King's
8. excursion
9. Reed Flute Cave
10. scenery

4
1. Sanya has a tropical climate.
   Xiamen has a subtropical monsoon climate.
   Dalian has a semi-moist monsoon climate and ocean climate features.
2. Located on the southern tip of Hainan Island, Sanya stands almost the same latitude as Hawaii. Thus, it's often called "the Hawaii of China" or "orient Hawaii".
3. Sanya has some of the most beautiful and well maintained stretches of sand not only in China but also in southern Asia. The sand there is white.
4. Its tourist attractions include Yalong Bay National holiday Resort, Dadonghai Tourist Zone, TianyaHaijiao, Luhuitou Park, Nanshan Cultural and Tourist Zone, the marvelous landscape of mountains and seas at Nanshan, Wuzhizhou Island, the Ancient City of Yazhou, Shuinan Village, Luobidong Cavern and the Muslim tombs built in Tang & Song dynasties, etc.
5. Xiamen has been nationally accredited as a Sanitary City, Model City for Environmental Protection, Garden City, and Excellence in Tourism City. It is generally acknowledged as one of the most livable cities in China and is commonly described as "a city on the sea and sea in the city".

6. Because the number of the pianos possessed is in the leading place in the nation, about 600, though there is only a population of 20,000 people. Also it is famous for being home to China's largest piano museum.
7. Xiamen has formed five main Tourist areas-Gulangyu Island Tourist Area, Nanputuo Temple Tourist Area, Wanshi Rock Tourist Area, Huangcuo Tourist Area and Jimei Tourist Area.
8. Bordered by the Bohai Sea and the Yellow Sea, Dalian is situated at the southern end of the Liaodong Peninsula in northeastern China.
9. One is Football and the other is Fashion.
10. Running from downtown Dalian there is a 40-kilometer road known as Binha winding along the coastline, northeast to southwest. This coastal area is a paradise for beach vacationers. The famous scenic spots of Bangchuidao Scenic Area, Laohutan Scenic Area, Jinshitan Scenic Area and Xinghai Square are scattered around this region. Situated in the central part of the southern seashore of Dalian City, Laohutan Ocean Park is the biggest modern lido in China.

5 1. Location 3. Characteristics 5. Tourist areas

7 1. Traditional Chinese medicine incorporates the Yin and Yang theory and the theory of the five elements.
2. Yin is the inner and negative principles, and Yang is the outer and positive. The five elements are metal, wood, water, fire, and the earth.
3. The people who feel uneasy and nervous may have too much Yang. Chinese doctors suggest them to eat more Yin foods like tofu.
4. Acupuncture is the insertion of very fine needles, on the body's surface, in order to influence physiological functioning of the body.
5. Sure we should.

Unit 10

Start-up

Pottery 陶器   Ivory carving 象牙雕刻   Porcelain 瓷器   Paper-Cut 剪纸
Lacquerware 漆器   Bonsai 盆景   Seal 图章

1 1. As we all know that tourism and shopping were not always balanced after all. Many tourists complain about too much shopping during a package tour. In my opinion, Shopping is as important as sightseeing to a tourist. When the tourist travels to a new destination, he or she wants to enjoy the local scenery, but also wants to know and to buy some typical local products at the same time. So when the local tour guide arranges the tour itinerary, the guide should balance shopping with sightseeing well.
2. The tour guide should tell the guest that the antiques which bought from a native people will be confiscated at the border. So the tour guide should suggest the guest to buy au-

thentic antiques which have been labeled as antiques from government owned store.

3. As a tour guide, you should not say "yes" or "no" when a tourist asks you such a question., because you can not make a decision for the tourist. You can only give some related information about the goods, and the best answer is to say "let's play it by ear".

4. The tour guide should remind the tourists of the following: 1) The meeting time and place. 2) Goods of each floor. 3) The style of payment in the store. 4) The way of packaging or airmail of the goods bought by any guest. 5) the telephone number or the name of the next destination in case of missing any tourist. 6) Keep reminding the group members of their personal and property safety.

5. The typical arts and crafts of China are embroidery, pottery, cloisonné, metalwork, lacquer ware, jade carving, furniture design, ivory carving, and textiles.

2
1. looking for	2. mail	3. lukewarm	4. reign
5. holds	6. fabrics	7. variety	8. cash
9. wrap	10. invoice		

4
1. The tour guide should bid farewell to the tourists fifteen minutes before reaching to the airport or railway station.

2. The tour guide should graciously deny any request that might delay the scheduled tour or departure. If there is plenty of time in the schedule, a tour guide may agree to the request and may even recommend good shops.

3. For domestic flights, the group should arrive at the airport 90 minutes in advance while for international flights, 120 minutes is needed before the plane takes off.

4. A tour guide should advise the tourist to go shopping in the antique shops and keep the invoice for the customs. A guide should also inform the tourist that the antique sold by peddlers usually do not carry a sign of authenticity, and tourists may not be able to take them out of China.

5. A tour guide should double check the plane tickets. For a domestic flight, the tour guide should check the date, flight schedule, flight number on the ticket. For an international flight, reconfirmation is needed apart from checking the above-mentioned items; if the plane tickets are not available before taking the tour, stay in touch with the travel service before, during and after the sightseeing for further information. The tour guide should contact with the airport to find out if there is any change of the flight schedule and arrange sufficient time for going to the airport. The activities before going to the airport should be well arranged. A short time visiting are strongly suggested. The tourists should not be left on their own, for they may get lost or miss their plane.

6. The local guide should help the tourist to look for the luggage and take the tourist to the lost-and-found office to register lost property. The tourist should specify the exterior characteristics of the luggage and the pieces of the luggage, and leave a phone number for further contact.

    The guide should also write down the address and phone number of the airline of-

fice and of the lost-and-found office at the airport, as well as the name of the person in charge. In this way, the guide can keep contact with the people concerned for further information during the tour. The passengers who lost the luggage may buy some daily necessities and submit receipts for reimbursement according to the regulations of the airline company.
7. The tourist should pay for the departure tax by themselves at the airport.
8. Omit.
9. Omit.
10. Omit.

5 3. Express the sad feeling to parting friends
4. Ask for advices and suggestions
5. Apologize for the unsatisfying service
6. Express the good blessings
8. Thank everyone again for the great co-operations

7 1. The best representatives of all the Chinese arts and crafts are Chinese painting, cloisonné and porcelain in your opinion.
2. Yes, I do. Such as porcelain, painting, paper-cut, seals, bonsai, silk flowers, kites and cloisonné.
3. Yes, jade is associated with merit, morality, grace and dignity in China.
4. I'm especially interested in Chinese Porcelain. Chinese Porcelain is also named "China", featuring its delicate texture, brilliant luster, pleasing color, and refined sculpture, has been one of the earliest artworks introduced to the western world through the Silk Road.
5. Sure. We should protect intellectual property and strengthen industrial supervision so as to maintain the market order of Chinese traditional arts and crafts and promote their continuous development.